Unveiling the Truth about Male Anatomy

Charlottx Z. Brooks

<u>***Funny helpful tips:***</u>

Invest in research and development; innovation drives business growth.

Your essence is a gift; share it generously with the world.

Unveiling the Truth about Male Anatomy : Unveiling the Enigma: A Revelatory Guide to Men's Body, Dispelling Myths & Celebrating Self-Acceptance

<u>**Life advices:**</u>

Understand each other's love languages; it enhances connection and intimacy.

Every setback is an opportunity in disguise; approach it with curiosity and a growth mindset.

Introduction

As we embark on this book, our goal is to approach this topic with a scientific and informative perspective. This guide aims to provide a comprehensive understanding of various aspects related to penis size and dispel common misconceptions.

Throughout this guide, we will explore different dimensions of penis size, including erect and flaccid measurements. We will also delve into the significance of girth and how it contributes to sexual satisfaction. Our approach will be objective and based on scientific methodologies to ensure accuracy and reliability.

It's important to address common myths and assumptions about penis size, as well as the impact of aging on the male reproductive organ. We will also explore the concept of "growers" and "show-ers" to better understand variations in penis appearance.

Additionally, we will discuss the concept of a micropenis, offering insights into this condition and potential treatment options. Our focus is to provide factual information, promote body positivity, and empower individuals to embrace their bodies and feel confident in their intimate relationships.

By the end of this guide, readers will gain a deeper understanding of penis size, debunking myths, and embracing the natural diversity that exists among men. Remember that communication, trust, and understanding are key elements in any intimate relationship, and size should never define one's self-worth. Let this book serve as a reliable source of knowledge and a resource for promoting healthy conversations about this topic.

Contents

Part I: The State of the Johnson

1

Loch Ness Johnson

As I mentioned in the introductory chapter, the primary reason for men's foundering johnson size confidence is a dearth of credible information. As a result, the majority of men's views on penis size are being warped by biased and incorrect information. It reminds me of the old adage: "in the absence of truth, the informational vacuum gets filled with heaps of bullshit." I may not have that completely right, but you get the point.

Why is finding information on something as fundamental as men's johnson sizes so difficult? The majority of sex researchers and medical professionals conducting these studies aren't incompetent. Unfortunately, the johnson has proven to be such a difficult organ to study because of some undeniable realities:

1) It's really difficult to get a large group of guys to voluntarily drop their drawers to get their most sensitive body part measured by a stranger with rubber gloves.

Most men abhor even getting undressed for the doctor during their annual physical. Because of this, it's difficult for researchers to find enough volunteers for studies on penis size. Most studies get stuck with small sample sizes, which reduce the accuracy and precision of a data set. Small samples also reduce the statistical power of a study, which makes it more difficult to draw any meaningful conclusions.

2) It's much easier for researchers to get men to volunteer for penis size studies if the subjects are allowed to measure themselves in the privacy of their homes. The only problem is that guys have a tendency to over-exaggerate everything.

The benefit of having test subjects self-measure is that it's much easier and cheaper to amass a large number of volunteers, but you're relying on guys to properly measure and report something they lie about constantly. Men are notorious for exaggerating everything: like how many people they've slept with, their height, how much alcohol they can drink, and their income. So what realistic chance do researchers have of getting a group of male test subjects to be objective?

The numbers back up this notion. A comparison of prominent self-measured versus independently measured studies on penis size shows that the self-reported studies report an average erect penis length about 2-3 cm (1") longer.

Size inflation has not been observed in self-measured studies on erect penis girth or circumference; at least not nearly to the same extent as length. This might be due to the fact that *length* is the prevailing penile dimension discussed among friends and in popular culture. Also, most people seem to have 6 inches anchored in their minds as the average male penis length despite dubious evidence. Penis width does not have any collectively anchored assumptions about what constitutes 'average'. I would venture a guess that the majority of people couldn't provide a good estimate of the average penis girth without using their hands.

3) Guys who are more confident in their penis size are more likely to volunteer to have their penis size measured. Guys who feel like they have a small johnson are less likely to volunteer for studies.

A 2001 study sponsored by Lifestyles condoms garnered a lot of attention for its flashy methods. The organizers set up a tent set outside a club in Mexico during spring break and asked for men to volunteer to have their erect johnson measured by qualified medical professionals.

Either because of the pressure, the copious amounts of alcohol consumed, or both, 25 percent of the men had to be eliminated from the study because they couldn't gain a strong enough erection for measurement.

Although the remaining 75 percent of erect penises were independently measured, the circumstances surrounding how the study obtained their volunteers, along with the significantly longer average length obtained as compared to more reputable studies, leads me to believe that the results are biased. Unless the researchers were able to measure each and every guy as they exited the club (they weren't), it's safe to assume that only the guys feeling cocksure about their erect cock size volunteered.

4) There is another group of men pretty agreeable to having their penis johnson size measured. It's the men already seeing urologists for other issues.

The problem is that this group of men doesn't represent the penis size distribution of normal, healthy men. Different urological conditions and ailments can affect penis size like Peyronie's disease, penile disease, prostate surgery, and erectile dysfunction.

*5) An already highly uncomfortable situation goes next level awkward when we're talking about measuring **erect** johnsons. A man needs to get himself in a certain frame of mind to be turned on enough for his penis to become erect. A doctor touching a man's erect penis while he's in that state of mind is potentially unsettling and may require years of psychotherapy to undo. That's an exaggeration of course, but it's a situation most men would prefer to avoid. That is unless the doctor looks like Dr. Quinn: Medicine Woman. That Jane Seymour is a minx! Erections are very fickle and fleeting. How do physicians and researchers know they are getting a man's best, or normal erection in such a johnson-softening i.e. unsexy environment?*

To overcome some of the problems described above, laboratory erections can be obtained with injections of prostaglandin E1, which is a vasodilator i.e. it widens blood vessels. A johnson can be topped up with some shots of phentolamine or papaverine if needed to ensure a full erection. The injection of vasodilators into the penis to induce an erection has been used as an effective treatment for erectile dysfunction dating back almost two decades *before* Viagra's (i.e. 20 BV) heavenly creation. Unlike Viagra, these injections act directly on the blood vessels to generate an erection regardless of arousal level, whereas Viagra mixes a potent physiological cocktail that needs an arousal spark for it to work.

Because of the myriad of erection related challenges, most studies throw in the towel and use the *stretched* johnson instead. Obtaining a stretched johnson measurement involves stretching the flaccid penis as much as possible without causing pain. It's been shown to be a decent proxy for erect penis length, but it's not accurate enough to be used reliably in my opinion. There's simply too many variables influencing the stretching procedure and it remains fundamentally different than your classic blood-filled erection. Also, stretched circumference can't be used as a proxy for erect circumference since the penis is only being stretched lengthwise.

Stretching a flaccid johnson from the sides would be tedious for the stretcher and just plain torturous for the strechee! Nevertheless, because of the lower difficulties to obtain, almost all of the published studies on male johnson size use either the flaccid or stretched penis.

The 6 Inch Assumption

If you ask people what they think the average erect penis length is, they will most likely say 6 inches, which is about 15.2 cm. When I ask people why they think it's 6 inches, I get a lot of shrugs and apathetic expressions. Before I performed any actual research, I would've said 6 inches as well. Why did I think that? Because that's the number I'd heard so I just assumed it was right. It's a round number after all, it must be right! But where does the well entrenched 6 inch assumption actually originate? It must've come from somewhere.

In 1948, the sex research pioneer Alfred Kinsey published the first known study on erect penis length. The sample size was large, as Kinsey obtained johnson measurements from over 2,500 American college students. The mean non bone-pressed erect penis length was 15.8 cm (6.2"), with almost two-thirds of the men falling between 5.5 and 6.5 inches. After this bellwether study, nothing else of consequence was published on johnson size for over 40 years!

The paucity of other studies and the notoriety of Alfred Kinsey led to his data becoming the standard. This is most certainly why 6 inches became anchored in the public's mind as the average male erect penis length.

A histogram reproduced from the Kinsey data (Gebhard et al, 1979) is presented in Figure 1.

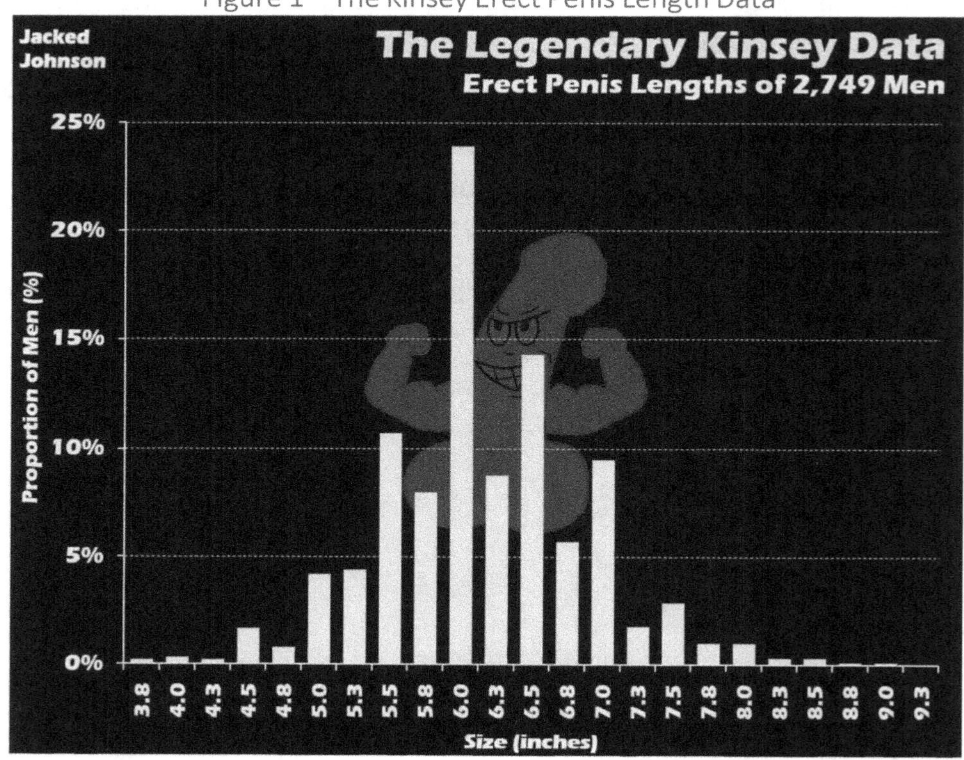

My issue with the Kinsey data is that the men self-measured their johnsons. The researchers gave each man a pre-stamped card to take home to mark off their flaccid and erect lengths. The self-measurement bias is the primary reason I don't include the Kinsey study in my data distributions.

In the next chapter, I'll walk you through the methodology and criteria for study inclusion for the johnson length and circumference data distributions.

2

How to Measure a Johnson

Since a definitive penis size study doesn't exist (because of some the reasons I described in the previous chapter), I guess it's up to me to make chicken salad out of chicken shit as they say and construct one. The good news is, after sifting through a lot of chicken shit I was able to find several well executed studies with only minor but very manageable flaws.

Combining data from multiple sources for analysis is called a *meta-analysis*. Meta-analysis is great because you don't actually have to get your hands dirty! In other words, I don't have to actually touch any dicks, which is a plus. Not that there's anything wrong with that. It's just not my thing.

The downside of meta-analysis is that the researcher is using second hand data from multiple sources, so additional uncertainty is being injected into the procedure. This is due to the fact that the meta-analyzer wasn't actually present for the data collection or the original analysis. In my case, I'm comfortable with this risk because:

1. I don't want to touch any dicks.

2. By combining different studies conducted by different individuals, the previously mentioned minor flaws from each individual study (e.g. small sample size, concentrated age groups/ethnicities) will hopefully offset each other or at least be reduced.

The key is to meta-analysis is to be strict with the type of studies that you include. Let me walk you through the first and most important part of the criteria.

How to Measure a Johnson

What if I told you that no standards for penile measurement actually exist? Yes, it's true, and it's a significant reason for the unfortunate situation we currently find ourselves in. How would you measure it? If you're a man, you probably already have. It seems like a simple enough process to perform but believe me, there's a myriad of variations that cause a calamity of confusion.

A set of quasi-standards emerged in a 1996 study published in the Journal of Urology (Wessells et al, 1996) titled, "Penile Length in the Flaccid and Erect States: Guidelines for Penile Augmentation." This is the gold standard of penis measurement studies, and in my opinion, its techniques should be universally adopted. The only flaws preventing this study from standing on its own as the definitive penis length authority are its small sample size of only 80 men and the older average age of its participants.

One of the key insights that the Wessells et al. study revealed was the difference between the two main methods to measure male johnson length:

1. Bone-pressed length (BPL)

2. Non bone-pressed length (NBPL)

The acronyms representing the two methods are strewn across message boards on penis enlargement sites but are much less known outside of that community. If you're not a visitor to these sites, you might be confused by exactly which 'bone' is being pressed on. Did you guess the dick bone? Not quite.

The PUFA

Believe it or not, a significant portion of a man's penis can't be seen. That's right, almost half of the male johnson is actually inside his body. What a waste, right? The part of the penis that you can't see is tucked under the pelvis and attached to the pubic bone. There's actually an area on a man's body that influences how much of his johnson is visible and free to partake in all the fun activities it loves so much. The *suprapubic fat pad* or *pubic upper fat area (PUFA),* is exactly what it sounds like: a mound of fat located just above and behind the penis. To use a basketball analogy, it's like a backboard. To give you a visual, Figure 2 is a diagram of the PUFA that was clearly not drawn by a professional and instead by your cheap author in MS Paint.

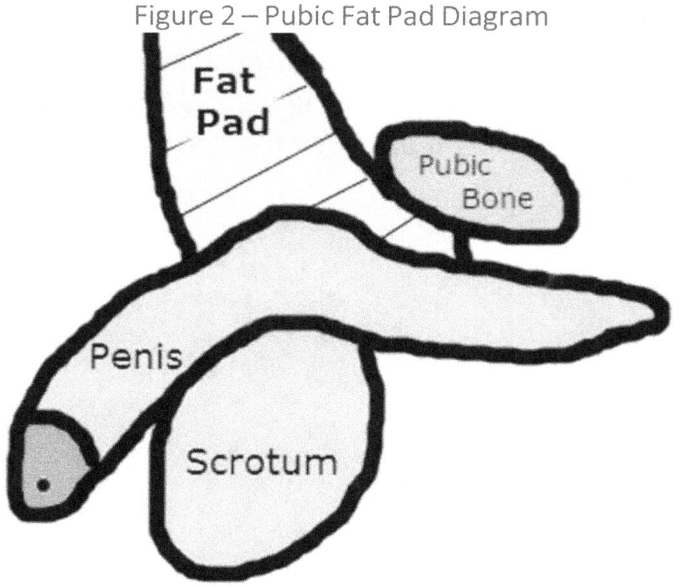

The Oak Tree

Think of a penis like a big oak tree with a large network of roots below the surface. That's how I like to think of mine. As a man puts on weight, he's effectively raising his soil level and burying more of his oak tree under the surface. If you don't care for my tree metaphor, as a man gains weight, his suprapubic area becomes thicker with fat and draws his penis inward. As if you needed more reasons to stay in shape! Dr. Mehmet Oz famously declared on Oprah! that a man losing 35 pounds of body weight could increase his penis length by one inch. That is insanity. I know guys who would cut off three or four toes to gain an inch of penis length.

To remove the influence of body fat and to measure a man's 'full' johnson length, some studies will press down on the fat pad and start measuring from the pubic bone (hence 'bone pressed length'). I'm not a fan of BPL as the primary johnson measurement technique. Now, it's perfectly fine and useful to measure a man's johnson in that manner. In some cases, it's important to remove the influence a man's body fat level has over his penis length. For example, it makes sense to use BPL if you want to do specific johnson size comparisons such as comparing penis size across different ages, ethnicities, or before and after an enlargement procedure.

Why don't I agree with bone-pressed length being used as the primary johnson measurement? I mean, I have a beautiful set of abs, but they just happen to be buried under some stomach fat. Do I still get credit for having a six pack? No! The portion of a man's johnson buried under his fat pad can't be seen by him or his partners. It's unusable, so there's no point in giving him credit for it.

The measurement technique I prefer measures from the base of the penis called the pubopenile skin junction. The BPL and NBPL techniques are displayed in another diagram that looks like it was drawn with crayons by a 4 year old child (Figure 3).

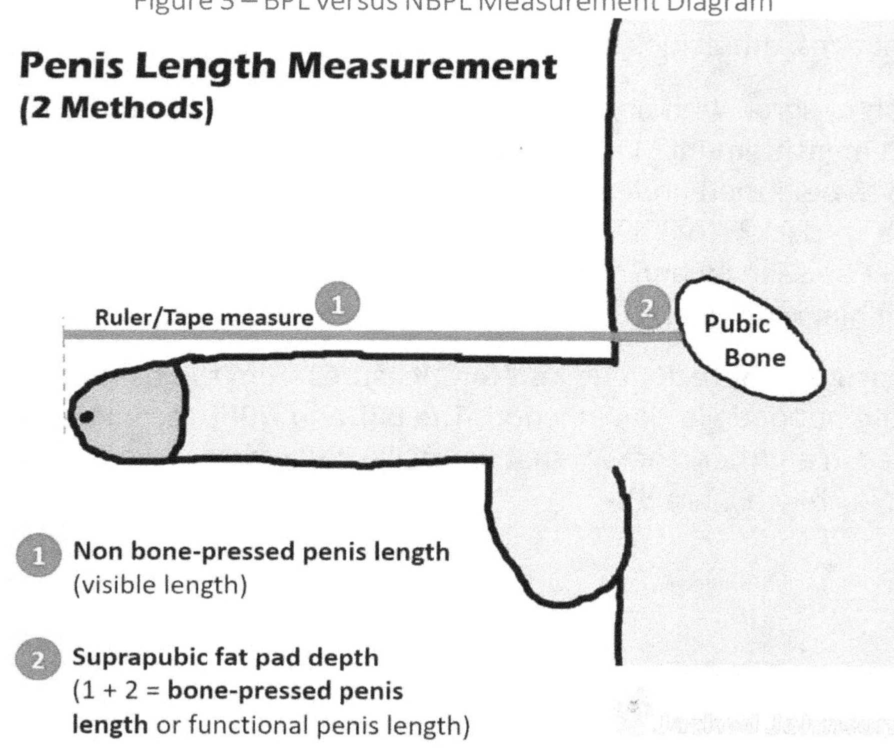

Confusing non bone-pressed and bone-pressed length is a common mistake found in studies or meta-analyses on penis length. A man's bone-pressed length will obviously be longer, but by how much exactly?

Two prominent johnson size studies measured the suprapubic fat pad depths of its participants. A summary of the data is displayed in Figure 4.

Jacked Johnson	**How Much Johnson Are We Hiding?**						
					Suprapubic Fat Pad Depth		
Study	Country	Sample Size	Age	Mean	S.D.	Min	Max
Wessells et al. (1996)	USA	80	54	2.9	1.6	0.5	7.5
Park et al. (1998)	Korea	309	41	2.3	0.7	1.0	4.5
Summary (cm)		389	48	2.6	1.6	0.5	7.5
Summary (inches)		389	48	1.0	0.6	0.2	3.0

The average fat pad depth across both studies is 2.6 cm or just over an inch. An extra inch being added to penis length data without proper explanation has definitely played a role in perpetuating men's collective johnson size anxiety.

The 'Fat American/Skinny Asian' stereotype plays itself out in the results, as the mean fat pad from the Wessells et al. study is 26 percent larger than Park et al., which is based out of Korea. I'll support my fellow North American men and note that the Park et al. participants are 13 years younger on average, and as we know men tend to pack on the pounds as they get older, especially in the stomach region.

The good news is that there's a lot of variability in the results. Pubic fat pad depths range from less than a centimeter to 7.5 cm, which is almost the size of an average flaccid johnson! If you're overweight, there literally could be an entire penis hiding inside you. It turns out that for guys with thicker than average fat pads, the best penis enlargement exercise doesn't actually involve the penis at all. The more you know.

Methodology Overview

The criteria I used for study inclusion and subsequent distribution creation is similar to the methodology followed by Veale et al. in a 2014 study published in the British Journal of Urology (Veale et al, 2014).

First of all, studies were excluded if there was any possible bias in penis size measurements, either because of the composition of the study's sample, or the measurement procedure. Studies were excluded if a study's participants had:

1. Any congenital or acquired penile abnormality (e.g. Peyronie's disease, hypospadias, intersex, hypospadias, phimosis, penile cancer, previous penile or prostatic surgery)

2. A complaint of small penis size or seeking augmentation

3. Erectile dysfunction

4. A self-measurement reading rather than a measurement taken by a health professional

5. Measurements made from cadavers

To be included, studies had to satisfy the following criteria:

1. Penis size was measured by a health professional

2. Participants were at least 17 years old

3. Mean and standard deviation of the sample size measurements were provided

4. Flaccid or erect length was measured from the base of the penis (pubo-penile junction) to the tip of the glans (meatus) on the dorsal (top) surface

5. Flaccid or erect circumference was measured at the base or mid-shaft of the penis and not from the corona/head/tip

You may have noticed that I didn't stipulate anything about measurement tools. There's some debate in the penis enlargement community whether a tape measure or ruler should be used to measure a johnson or if it even matters at all. You definitely hear more clamouring for tape measurements from the dudes with curvy penises! The reason is best explained by another one of my beautiful diagrams, shown in Figure 5.

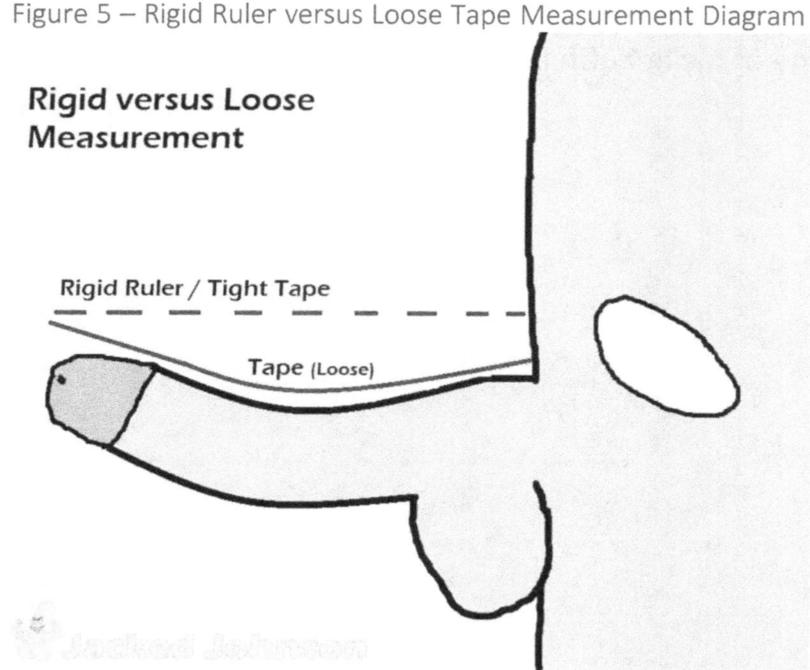

The Trouble with the Curve

You can see how guys with curved erect johnsons get potentially shortchanged if a rigid measurement device is used. An erect johnson can curve up, down, to the right, to the left, or have a combo curve! One thing is for sure, curved johnsons are very common. A 1997 study by Joseph Sparling (Sparling, 1997) found that only 54 percent of its participants had straight erect johnsons. 'U-curved' johnsons, johnsons that curve up to the sky like the letter U, were observed in almost 1 out of 4 men. Downwards curving johnsons, called 'on-curved', were found in almost 1 out of 6 men.

I call downward curving johnsons 'doggy style dicks' because the vagina's slight upwards curve towards a woman's belly button will actually shape a man's johnson slightly downward in the doggy style position. A u-curve is more likely to be forged with a woman on top position. I'm not saying position preference and a lady's honey pot cause penile curvature. The upwards curve in most vaginas is minor and the organ itself is very malleable. But a lot of repeated exposure to a certain position or penile injuries sustained in certain positions can definitely make a man more likely to get a johnson curve. I mean, how many pornstars have curved johnsons? You see a lot of the right and left curved johnsons in porn. By the way, the same study found 14 percent and 1 percent of men had left and right curved erect johnsons respectively. The much higher left curve proportion versus right is difficult to explain. Especially considering most men are right handed.

The johnson curve measurement conundrum is similar to the measurement of height for people with curved spines or kyphosis, which is excess spinal curvature. If Kyphosis sufferers didn't have a curved spine, they would obviously be taller when measured vertically in a straight line. But we don't measure height with a loose tape measure, tracing along the curve of people's backs, so why do it for johnsons?

In my opinion, it comes down to *functionality* or *usability*. Height or stature by definition is vertical distance off the ground, not the length of your body. A Kyphosis sufferer's eyes and arms drop to lower levels and as a result, they don't have the same practical usability of their body length as people with the same body length but that stand taller.

For the johnson, you also want to capture its *functional* size. Let's face it, the johnson size game is about taking up as much space as possible in whatever orifice it's in. Even if a johnson is curved and doesn't span out horizontally from the body as much as it would if it were perfectly straight, the fully curved length adds to its overall size and thus should be counted. Therefore, as a proud owner of a slightly u-curved johnson which in no way influenced my opinion, I prefer the loose tape measurement technique.

I see the other side of the argument though. The depth of penile thrusts on a curved johnson would arguably be slightly deeper if it were perfectly straight. If a curved johnson and straight erect johnson both measured 14 cm in length with the loose tape technique, the straight johnson could argue it can actually thrust 14 cm deep into a lady's love tunnel, while the curved johnson might not quite reach that far. Both johnsons take up the exact same amount of space, which is the determining factor in my opinion.

So my official stance is that I prefer loose tape measurement, but I didn't exclude studies that used a rigid measurement technique. From what I observed in studies using both techniques, the results are impacted negligibly; definitely not enough for me to omit any studies that used one technique over another. Remember that men with Peyronie's disease, erect penises that bend severely to the point it often causes pain during sex, aren't included in my data.

For erect johnson length, four published studies survived the gauntlet I laid out above. I decided to weigh each of the four equally at 25 percent each, instead of weighing by sample size like I've seen in other meta-analysis studies. I did this to minimize measurement bias from an individual study disproportionally affecting the overall results. I followed the same procedure for the flaccid johnson data.

Next, I calculated the weighted mean and pooled standard deviation of the group of studies. From there, the final step was to randomly simulate a large normal distribution of 20,000 data points, or in our case 20,000 johnsons. Using the pooled summary statistics from studies to simulate a very large sample smooths out the distribution. This makes it much easier to analyze and display.

The end goal of following this methodology is to end up with the largest, most accurate, and most beautiful nomogram to display the distribution of johnson size dimensions. A nomogram is the most effective way of displaying data by percentile. The more statistically inclined reader might know nomograms by its other name, a cumulative distribution function or CDF.

An example of a nomogram is shown in Figure 6.

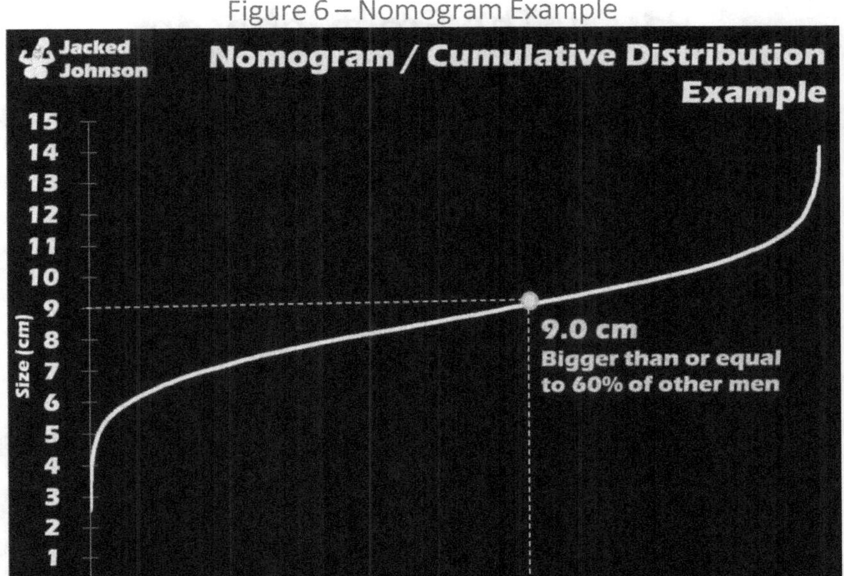

Nomograms (in the manner they're being presented here) are made up of a set of values being measured on one axis (e.g. johnson length, test scores, height) and its associated percentile on the other axis. Just like with test scores or income, you want to be in a high percentile, which tells you how many other people in the group being evaluated you are equal to or higher than. Just select a size value from one axis and observe at which percentile the line crosses through on the other. For example, if a johnson size nomogram says you're in the 80th percentile, you're the same size or larger than 80 percent of men, or 4 out of 5 men. Nice!

In the next chapter, I'll take you through the studies that made the cut for erect johnson length and present the data distribution.

Part II: The Erect Johnson

3

Blowing Up the 6 Inch Assumption: Erect Johnson Length

Like I mentioned in the previous chapter on methodology, just four studies made the cut to be part of the most accurate and robust erect penis size data set the world has ever known.

The following is an overview of the four studies included in the erect penis length distribution.

1) *Penile Length in the Flaccid and Erect States: Guidelines for Penile Augmentation. Wessells, Hunter et al. (1996). USA.*

The first study to make the cut is the previously mentioned 1996 American study from led by Hunter Wessells. Eighty physically normal men's johnsons were evaluated in the flaccid, stretched and erect states. The majority of the participants were white (54), with 16 being African American and 10 Asian. The average age of the men was a bit on the older side, coming in at 54. Erections were obtained via intracavernous injection of prostaglandin E1 and some good old fashioned self-stimulation. Mean erect penis length was 12.89 cm (5.1"). Even with a relatively small number of participants, there was a wide range of results, with the shortest erect johnson measuring 7.5 cm (3") and the longest 19.0 cm (7.5"). I mentioned this earlier but it bears repeating: this is the gold standard of penis measurement studies to which all others should be... measured.

2) *Penile length and circumference: an Indian study. Promodu et al. (2007). India.*

Measured 301 physically normal Indian men's johnsons in the flaccid and stretched states, but only 93 in the erect state. Mean age of participants was 32 years old. Interestingly, the researchers had 93 participants self-report their erect length and circumference and then chose 50 from that same group to be subsequently measured by investigators. This exercise was undertaken to investigate potential bias in self-reported numbers. This was an interesting manoever, as how much would the men exaggerate if they knew there was a fifty-fifty chance that they were going to get measured by somebody else and be proven a liar? No one likes to look foolish like that. The results proved that out, as the traditional upward bias seen in self-measured figures effectively disappeared. The mean erect length of self-measured subjects was 13.01 cm (5.1"), which was only slightly more than the 12.93 cm (5.1") reported by investigators and not statistically significant. The standard deviations were virtually identical. Erections were obtained the good old fashioned way, with the help of a 'videotape'; were VCRs even still around in 2007? Men were excluded if they didn't achieve a full erection so only 41 fully erect johnsons ended up being measured by an investigator. That's obviously a very low sample size, but the fact that the results were virtually identical to the self-measurement sample of 93 men and the techniques were sound, I felt confident including this study.

3) *Erect Penile Dimensions in a Cohort of 778 Middle Eastern Men: Establishment of a Nomogram. Habous, Mohamad et al. (2015). Saudi Arabia.*

A study of the penis length of 778 physically normal men (mean age 43.7; range 20 to 82) attending urological outpatient clinics in Saudi Arabia. Erection was induced using an intracavernosal injection of Quadrimix. Mean erect penis length was 12.53 cm (4.9") with a standard deviation of 1.93 cm (0.8"). The shortest penis was measured to be 4.0 cm (1.6") and the longest was 18.0 cm (7.1"). Participants were excluded if they presented a complaint of small or short penis, Peyronie's disease or complaint of congenital curvature, clinical hypogonadism, and previous penile surgery or trauma.

4)   Penile Nomogram in Korean Males. Park, K et al. (1998). Korea.

The study measured 309 men's johnsons in the flaccid, stretched and erect states. Erections were induced via injection of prostaglandin E1 and self-stimulation. This study is basically a Korean version of the Wessells et al. study, as it followed its methodology step by step. Mean erect penis length was 11.88 cm (4.7"), which was the shortest figure out of the four included studies, and over 1 cm shorter than the Wessells study. Let the 'Asians have smaller penises' speculation reignite! Before you non-asians get carried away, keep in mind the Park et al. study alone is not definitive enough to draw the 'Asians have smaller johnsons' conclusion. Additional statistically sound evidence is required and comparisons would need to take place *within* the same study to minimize measurement bias.

I decided to weigh each of the four studies 25 percent each instead of weighing by sample size. I did this to minimize measurement bias from an individual study disproportionally affecting the overall results. Also, since the goal is to replicate the global mean erect penis length, weighing each study individually creates a favourable racial distribution on par with the global population.

Figure 7 displays how the race distribution shakes out for erect johnson length data.

Erect Penis Size - Summary of Studies Used			
Race	% of World Population	J.J. Distribution	Difference
East Asian	25%	28%	3%
Central / South Asian	23%	25%	3%
European	15%	17%	1%
African	12%	5%	-7%
Near Eastern	11%	25%	14%
Mixed	5%	0%	-5%
Oceanian	3%	0%	-3%
Native American	1%	0%	-1%
Other	5%	0%	-5%
Total	100%	100%	0%

Not bad right? Despite the low number of studies available from any country, the size distribution I'm going to present you shortly is roughly in line with the global racial composition. The Wessells et al. study, despite being conducted in the US, broke down the race of its participants as 68 percent white, 12 percent Asian and 20 percent African so I was able to group these men as well.

Figure 8 displays a summary of the studies.

JJ	Erect Penis Length - Summary of Studies Used						
Study	Country	Sample Size	Age	Mean	S.D.	Min	Max
Wessells et al. (1996)	USA	80	54	12.89	2.91	7.5	19.0
Promodu et al. (2007)	India	41	32	12.93	1.63	10.5	17.0
Habous et al. (2015)	Saudi Arabia	778	44	12.53	1.93	4.0	18.0
Park et al. (1998)	Korea	309	36	11.88	1.32	7.5	17.6
Summary (cm)		1208	41	12.56	1.95	4.0	19.0
Summary (inches)		1208	41	4.94	0.77	1.6	7.5

all measurements non bone pressed

Forget about six inches, with an overall mean of 12.56 cm, the average erect penis length is under five inches! I was shocked at these results, and they should come as a great relief to a lot of men. It's pretty incredible that the 6 inch stereotype has been allowed to perpetuate for as long as it has in light of these results from legitimate sources.

None of the four included studies have a mean erect length even close to 6 inches (15.2 cm). In fact, based on the overall distribution created from the data, not even 1 in 10 men has an erect johnson that long or longer! Overall standard deviation came in at 1.95 cm or 0.8 inches. Since the data is normally distributed, this means roughly two-thirds of men have an erect penis length between 10.6 cm (4.2") and 14.5 cm (5.7").

Figure 9 is a histogram of the data.

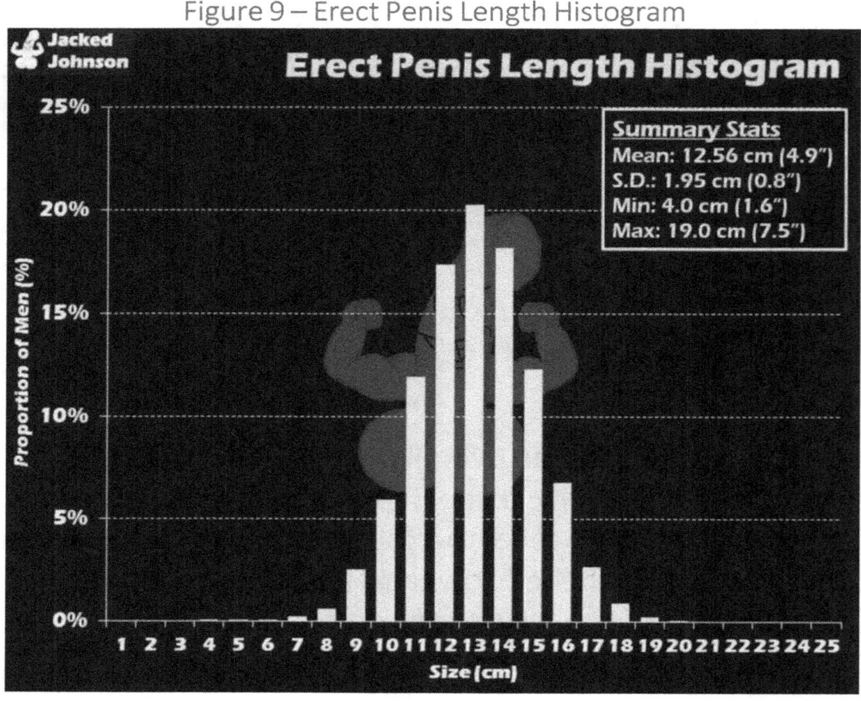

Now that you finally know what the 'true' average erect johnson length is, I'm sure you're now wondering what everyday items are closest in size to it. I know that's what I wondered. Figure 10 displays a length comparison of the mean erect johnson. Apologies in advance if I've ruined these items for you forever.

Jacked Johnson
Is that a can of soda in your pocket?
Erect Penis Size Comparisons

Object	Length (cm)	Length Difference (absolute)
Erect Penis	12.6	
US Dollar Bill	15.6	3.0
Standard Pen	14.5	1.9
iPhone 6/6S	13.8	1.3
Male Hand	18.9	6.3
Banana	19.0	6.4
Cucumber	23.0	10.4
Red Bull Can (250mL)	13.4	0.8
Soda Can (355mL)	12.1	0.5
Sushi - California Roll	2.5	10.0
Kielbassa	17.0	4.4
Hotdog	15.2	2.7
Footlong Hotdog	30.5	17.9

I've heard guys talk about having a soda or pop can penis, but they say it to brag about their alleged massive girth. Now 'pop can penis' can take on a whole new meaning...of being average length. The slightly longer can of the popular energy drink Red Bull is also close, followed by the standard iPhone.

So next time you find yourself taking a 'dick pic' for that special someone, consider doing a quick length comparison with your device; you may reconsider sending it!

Johnson circumference, or girth, doesn't get nearly the same amount of attention or scrutiny as johnson length. This is the case despite mounting evidence that girth matters *more* in terms of delivering effective stimulation to the heterosexual man's target audience's spasm chasm. A prevailing reason for girth's increased importance comes down to the female pink fortress' design.

Most of the silk igloo's pleasure nerve endings are located in its inner one third near the opening (about the first two inches), so it makes sense for a woman to want to maximize the surface area contact a man provides to this area during intercourse. Also, a thicker johnson will cause more friction inside the vagina, which causes the skin around the all-important clitoris to move. This results in a more pleasurable experience...from what I've heard. Finally, women often describe the pleasurable sensations of feeling "full" with a thicker penis inside their love tunnel.

Six studies made the cut to be included in building the erect circumference distribution. Four of the studies were included in the erect length distribution, with two additions from Korea.

1) Penile Length in the Flaccid and Erect States: Guidelines for Penile Augmentation. Wessells, Hunter et al. (1996). USA.

2) Penile length and circumference: an Indian study. Promodu et al. (2007). India.

3) Erect Penile Dimensions in a Cohort of 778 Middle Eastern Men: Establishment of a Nomogram. Habous, Mohamad et al. (2015). Saudi Arabia.

4A) Penile Nomogram in Korean Males. Park, K et al. (1998). Korea.

The following two studies were not used for erect length because they used the bone-pressed method but are included for erect circumference.

4B) The Relationship between Height and Body Weight and Penis Size in University Students. Yoon, JS et al. (1998). Korea.

150 healthy young Korean men participated with an average age of 22. Mean erect circumference averaged 11.17 cm (4.4") with a standard deviation of 1.05 cm.

4C) A Study on the Penile Size of Korean Men. Kyoung Mo Cheung. (1971). Korea.

702 Korean males participated in this study with an age range of 21 to 31. Mean erect penis circumference was 11.0 cm (4.3") with a range of 9 cm to 15.5 cm.

The three Korean studies were weighted equally to maintain a favourable global participant distribution. The Korean average and the three other studies were then weighted equally at 25 percent each to create the overall average and standard deviation for erect circumference. A summary is shown in Figure 11.

JJ Erect Penis Circumference - Summary of Studies Used							
Study	Country	Sample Size	Age	Mean	S.D.	Min	Max
Wessells et al. (1996)	USA	80	54	12.30	1.31	9.0	16.0
Promodu et al. (2007)	India	41	32	11.49	1.04	9.0	13.5
Habous et al. (2015)	Saudi Arabia	778	44	11.50	1.74	5.0	16.0
3 Korean Studies	Korea	1161	29	11.43	1.08	7.5	15.5
Summary (cm)		**2060**	**40**	**11.68**	**1.29**	**5.0**	**16.0**
Summary (inches)		2060	40	4.60	0.51	2.0	6.3

The mean erect circumference is 11.68 cm or about 4.6 inches, with a range of 5 cm to 16 cm. Based on that figure, it appears that the average erect johnson is about 1 cm less in circumference than it is in length. Notice the much smaller standard deviation for girth as compared to length (1.29 cm versus 1.95 cm). Figure 12 presents a histogram of the distribution.

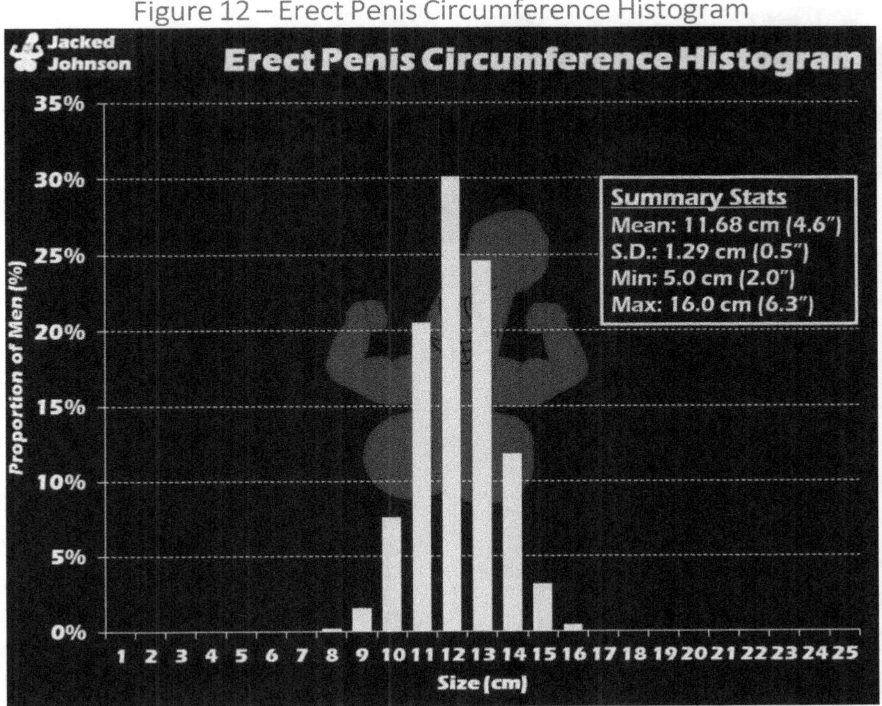

Figure 13 displays a comparison of everyday objects to the newly defined average erect johnson width. Again, apologies in advance if I've ruined these items for you.

Figure 13 – Erect Penis Circumference Comparison Chart

Jacked Johnson		
You'll Never Look at Sushi the Same Way Again		
Erect Penis Size Comparisons		
Object	Circumference (cm)	Width Difference (absolute)
Erect Penis	11.7	
US Dollar Bill	6.6	5.1
Standard Pen	2.1	9.6
Male Index Finger	8.2	3.5
Banana (unpeeled)	13.0	1.3
Cucumber	17.0	5.3
Red Bull Can (250mL)	16.9	5.2
Soda Can (355mL)	20.8	9.1
Sushi - California Roll	12.0	0.3
Kielbassa	14.2	2.5
Hotdog	4.3	7.4
Footlong Hotdog	4.9	6.8

A staple in most sushi meals (at least in North America) and one of my personal favourite foods, the California roll is the closest to the 11.7 cm circumference of the average erect penis. An unpeeled banana is next closest with a girth of 13 cm. The previously discussed soda/pop can, a preeminent johnson comparison in locker rooms all over the world, is almost double the girth of the real thing. This means that all of the pop can penis jokes are even more of an exaggeration than previously thought... but funny nonetheless and will continue to be used by this author.

5 Bananas, Soda Cans and Sushi

At this point, you should have a good feel for the erect johnson sizes being deployed in bedrooms around the globe. In this chapter, I'm going to bring the two dimensions together so that you can get a better sense of how they interact. We're obviously going to begin with a multi-dimensional comparison to everyday objects (Figure 14). Now we can determine the definitive johnson simulator!

Jacked Johnson	**Is that a can of Red Bull in your pocket?** Erect Penis Size Comparisons				
Object	Length (cm)	Circumference (cm)	Length Difference (absolute)	Width Difference (absolute)	Total Difference (cm)
Erect Penis	**12.6**	**11.7**			
US Dollar Bill	15.6	6.6	3.0	5.1	8.1
Standard Pen	14.5	2.1	1.9	9.6	11.5
Male Index Finger	8.6	8.2	4.0	3.5	7.4
Male Index+Middle Fingers	8.8	11.5	3.8	0.2	4.0
Male Thumb	7.9	9.1	4.7	2.6	7.2
Banana (unpeeled)	18.0	13.0	5.4	1.3	6.8
Cucumber	23.0	17.0	10.4	5.3	15.8
Red Bull Can (250mL)	13.4	16.9	0.8	5.2	6.0
Soda Can (355mL)	12.1	20.8	0.5	9.1	9.6
Sushi - California Roll	2.5	12.0	10.0	0.3	10.3
Kielbassa	17.0	14.2	4.4	2.5	7.0
Hotdog	15.2	4.3	2.7	7.4	10.1
Footlong Hotdog	30.5	4.9	17.9	6.8	24.7

You may have noticed that I added two new johnson simulators to the chart which are both hand related. Something men and women use every day to simulate a male johnson comes closest to the real thing. The classic index and middle finger combination, an indispensable technique in any man's vaginal foreplay repertoire, has the lowest absolute difference of length and width.

The two finger combination is admittedly the best penis simulator on the human body. There's even the added bonus of a free moving digit, the thumb, perfectly positioned to stimulate the clitoris while the index and middle do their thing. The johnson doesn't have a clit stimulating feature like that. The closest thing would be if a guy grew his pubic hair really long and braided it. But why would you do that? That's absurd...I've never tried it...it's ludicrous to even mention...look, it's competitive out there! We all need an edge! Leave me alone! The two finger combination also has that little pinky available if a man wants to try and sneak across the southern border.

The circumference value of the index/middle finger combination is a bit of 'fool's gold' since its shape is not cylindrical like a penis. Because of this, and because I'm a man of principles, I've disqualified it as the number one johnson simulator. That distinguished honour now goes to the banana, a.k.a. nature's dildo! Congratulations to the banana. The banana is long enough, hard enough and nearly the perfect width; it has it all! Including a severe case of upward-sloping Peyronie's disease.

Sizing up the Competition

Following the same train of thought, it's interesting to consider how the average johnson compares to actual johnson simulators a.k.a. dildos; manufactured items specifically designed to simulate or replace the real thing. I logged onto Amazon.com and pulled the specs on the three top selling dildos in America. This is something I've since come to regret, as I now get inundated weekly with 'You Might Be Interested In...' emails from Amazon that would make a pornstar blush.

To save you that embarrassment, I've listed the specs from the male johnson's top selling competition in Figure 15.

Figure 15 – Erect Penis Size versus Top Selling Dildos

Jacked Johnson	How Does the Real Thing Stack Up? Erect Penis Length vs Top Selling Dildos				
Object	Length (cm)	Circumference (cm)	Length Difference (absolute)	Width Difference (absolute)	Total Difference
Erect Penis	**12.6**	**11.7**	-	-	
Naughty Cock 6.5" Dildo	13.5	11.6	0.9	0.1	1.0
Xhivar Superior 7" Dildo	13.0	11.4	0.4	0.3	0.7
UTIMI 7" Silicone Dildo	13.5	12.5	0.9	0.8	1.7

Source: Amazon.com

Incredibly, top selling dildos are almost identically proportioned to the average male johnson. I was blown away by that...and somewhat relieved. The top two selling dildos are actually *thinner* than the average erect penis. Although all three products are advertised to be over 6.5 inches, the actual 'insertable' length is significantly less. If you're wondering how I know that, it's listed on the site, so save your jokes, smart ass!

Alright enough about johnson simulators, let's get back to the real thing. The histograms of erection length and circumference are shown in Figure 16.

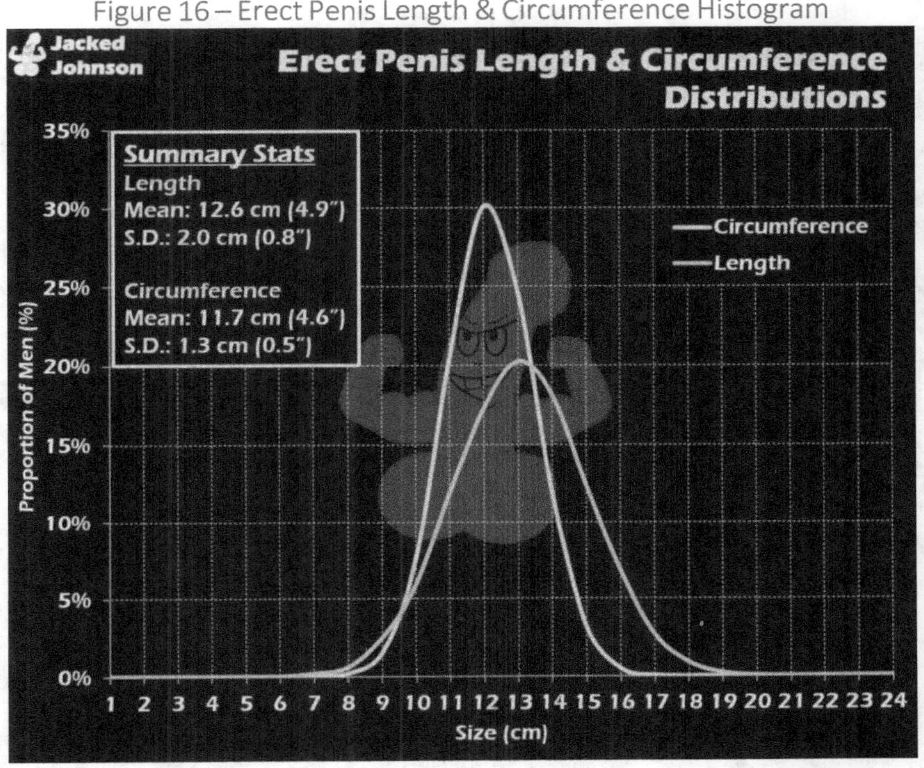

The bell curve of erect length is shifted over slightly to the right compared to circumference because its mean is 8 percent larger (12.56 cm versus 11.68 cm). What's also evident in the graph is length's much wider dispersion. This is because the standard deviation of erect length is 48 percent larger than erect girth (1.95 cm versus 1.29 cm). Figure 17 is a nomogram of erect length and circumference.

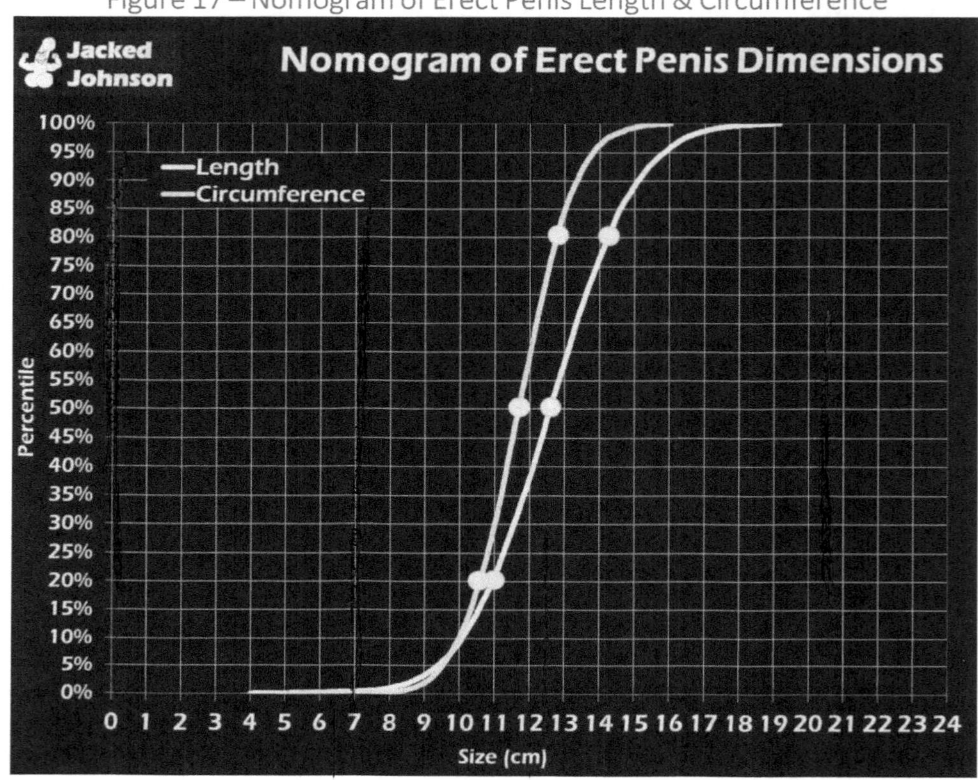

Roughly two-thirds of guys have erect johnson girths between 10.4 cm (4.1") and 13.0 cm (5.1"). Four out of five guys are between 10.0 cm (3.9") and 13.3 cm (5.2").

For length, two-thirds of men are between 10.7 cm (4.2") and 14.4 cm (5.7"). Four out of five guys are between 10.1 cm (4.0") and 15.1 cm (5.9"). Figure 18 is a chart to aid in the interpretation of the nomogram.

Jacked Johnson	Erect Penis Dimensions by Percentile		
Percentile	Explanation	Length	Circumference
10%	Bigger than or equal to 1 out of 10 guys	10.3 cm (4.1")	10.0 cm (3.9")
20%	Bigger than or equal to 1 out of 5 guys	11.0 cm (4.3")	10.6 cm (4.2")
30%	Bigger than or equal to 3 out of 10 guys	11.6 cm (4.5")	11.0 cm (4.3")
40%	Bigger than or equal to 2 out of 5 guys	12.1 cm (4.7")	11.3 cm (4.5")
50%	Bigger than or equal to 1 out of 2 guys	12.6 cm (4.9")	11.7 cm (4.6")
60%	Bigger than or equal to 3 out of 5 guys	13.1 cm (5.2")	12.0 cm (4.7")
70%	Bigger than or equal to 7 out of 10 guys	13.6 cm (5.4")	12.4 cm (4.9")
80%	Bigger than or equal to 4 out of 5 guys	14.2 cm (5.6")	12.8 cm (5.0")
90%	Bigger than or equal to 9 out of 10 guys	15.1 cm (5.9")	13.4 cm (5.3")
99%	Bigger than or equal to 99 out of 100 guys	17.1 cm (6.7")	14.7 cm (5.8")

Remarkably, having a 6 inch penis does not make you average, but puts you in the 90th percentile! That's funny because half the guys I've met in my life have claimed to have erect johnsons 6 inches long. I must hang with a lot of well-hung men...or they're liars. The penis size 'one-percent', society's phallic elite, is a mere 6.8 inches, or 17.3 cm. The girth/circumference numbers are even more eye opening. A girth just above 5 inches puts a man in the 90th percentile.

What if I told you that analyzing erect penis length and circumference is not the optimal way to quantify penis size? Yes, it's true. Since the male johnson is a three dimensional pleasure-producing, bodily fluid-shooting wonder, it's important to measure it in three dimensions. To accomplish this (in the next chapter), I'll dust off a geometry formula that I haven't used since grade school. I'm sure my grade 6 geometry teacher Mrs. Leonard will be proud.

6 3D J6hnson

The best way to measure the three-dimensional size of a johnson is to calculate its volume. If you recall from grade 6 geometry, volume measures how much space an object takes up, or how much you could theoretically fill an object up with a liquid if it was hollowed out. Some previously published studies on penis size have done this, using the volume formula for the johnson's closest shape, the cylinder. The formula isn't perfect, most notably because the johnson head is rounded like a muffin top and not flat, but it's an effective approximation.

Calculating penile volume is a great way to assess a man's *true* johnson size. Like I mentioned in an earlier chapter, the size game is about taking up as much space as possible. I also want to give the short but 'girthy' johnsons out there a fair shake. There's a lot of guys walking around feeling less than confident about their johnsons unaware of the fact that their girth puts their three dimensional size figure in good relative standing. Figure 19 is a diagram of a cylinder and the formula required to calculate its volume.

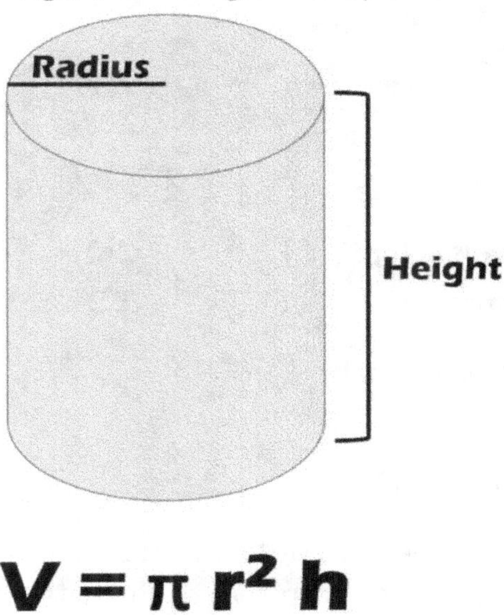

$$V = \pi r^2 h$$

I know complicated math formulas make most people's penises soft and brains hurt but it's actually pretty simple. You just multiply pi (approx. 3.14159) by the radius squared and the height. Height in our case is length. Since we don't have penile radius measurements, we'll convert the circumference values. The formula to convert circumference to radius is:

Radius = Circumference / 2π

Figure 20 is a summary of the average erect penis dimensions with its calculated penile volume.

| | The Average Erect Penis | | | |
| | Jacked Johnson Model | | | |
Measure	Size (cm)	Standard Deviation	Min	Max
Erect Penis Length	12.6	2.0	4.0	19.0
Erect Penis Circumference	11.7	1.3	5.0	16.0
Erect Penile Volume (cm^3)	137.0		8.0	387.4

Based on our derived length and circumference measurements, the average erect penis volume is about 137 cubic centimeters (cc) or cm^3. Since 1 cc is equal to 1 mL, it's intuitive to draw the conclusion that 137 cc of blood is required to create an average erection but that's not exactly true. The reason is that the penis isn't completely hollow. There's a lot of non-erectile tissue in there like the penile skin, urethra, subcutaneous tissue, tunica albuginea, and corpus spongiosum. The part that contains almost all of the blood during an erection is the corpora cavernosa, a set of cylindrical chambers made of spongy erectile tissue. So to accurately determine erectile blood volume, measuring the volume of the corpora is what's required; but you can't exactly measure that with a ruler!

My childlike computer drawings won't do something as intricate as the inside of a johnson justice, so if you're curious, a good diagram can be found by clicking on the link below.

Inside of a Johnson Diagram

Fortunately, since we're only interested in the *full* three dimensional size of a penis, our cylinder formula works just fine. The formula for the volume of a cylinder is going to tell us roughly how much space a johnson takes up in say, a vagina! Following that logic, the average male johnson takes up about 137 cc of space. Based on studies that have analyzed corpora cavernosa size, the ratio of the corpora volume to the full johnson volume is about 50 percent. That corresponds to a blood volume of about 70 cc for the average erect johnson.

Small changes in girth and length have a significant impact on penile volume. The smallest erect penis recorded in the studies I analyzed was about 4 cm long by 5 cm around, which results in a volume of about 8 cc; to give you a visual, a shot of alcohol is 30 cc. The largest penis recorded in any of the studies was about 19 cm by 16 cm, which equates to over 387 cc in volume; over 48 times larger than the smallest johnson. That's almost a full pint glass of dick! The average man has only ten pints of blood in his entire body, so guys fortunate enough to possess johnsons that size might be unconscious by the time the required half pint of blood fills it up. So...like...I don't envy them at all...poor bastards.

To aid in your understanding of how length and circumference impact johnson volume, I've created a chart that displays the approximate penile volume for given measurements in both dimensions (Figure 21). You'll see in the chart that changes in circumference have a more dramatic impact on penile volume than the equivalent change in length. This means that a johnson measuring 11 cm around and 10 cm long is going to have a larger volume than a johnson measuring 10 cm around and 11 cm long. The impact on volume or 3D size is yet another reason why girth is the dimension that should rule the day in terms of johnson size and not length! Your days are numbered skinny dicks!

One of the best examples of the concept I'm describing is a foot long hotdog. Your typical ballpark foot long hotdog is obviously a foot long (30.5 cm), which is a colossal length in the land of johnsons. You definitely don't want to be in a devil's threesome with a guy packing that! You'd be relegated to a masturbating spectator pretty quickly. But hold the phone, a typical foot long hot dog only measures 5 cm (2") around. Its proportionally scrawny width gives a foot long hot dog a volume of less than 60 cc! That's less than half the size of the average erect johnson.

You're back in the driver's seat of that devil's threesome with Mr. Footlong cock! Congratulations.

Marginal girth is more advantageous to a man's overall penis size than marginal length except for a few cases. Basically, unless a man's johnson is shaped like the famous boxer Eric "Butterbean" Esch, he's always going to be better off increasing it 1 cm in circumference versus 1 cm in length in terms of maximizing overall size. Butterbean dicks are pretty rare and most guys are clustered around the mean values. To aid in that visualization, I've overlaid a heat map on top of the previously mentioned volume chart which corresponds to the proportion of men with erect johnsons within a given range of volume values (Figure 21).

Jacked Johnson — **Erect Penis Volume by Circumference and Length**
volume measured in cm^3 (cc)

Erect Penis Circumference (cm and inches) — rows; Erect Penis Length (cm and inches) — columns.

in	cm\\cm	1	2	3	4	5	6	7	8	9	10	11	12	13	14	15	16	17	18	19	20	21	22	23	24
7.9	20	15	45	76	106	136	166	197	227	257	287	318	348	378	409	439	469	499	530	560	590	620	651	681	711
7.5	19	14	41	68	95	123	150	177	204	232	259	286	313	340	368	395	422	449	477	504	531	558	586	613	640
7.1	18	12	37	61	85	110	134	158	183	207	232	256	280	305	329	353	378	402	426	451	475	500	524	548	573
6.7	17	11	32	54	76	97	119	141	162	184	206	227	249	271	292	314	336	357	379	401	422	444	466	487	509
6.3	16	10	29	48	67	86	105	124	143	163	182	201	220	239	258	277	296	315	335	354	373	392	411	430	449
5.9	15	8	25	42	59	75	92	109	125	142	159	176	192	209	226	243	259	276	293	310	326	343	360	376	393
5.5	14	7	22	36	51	65	80	94	109	123	138	152	167	181	196	210	225	239	254	268	283	297	312	326	341
5.1	13	6	19	31	44	56	68	81	93	106	118	131	143	155	168	180	193	205	218	230	242	255	267	280	292
4.7	12	5	16	26	37	47	58	68	79	89	100	111	121	132	142	153	163	174	184	195	205	216	226	237	247
4.3	11	4	13	22	31	39	48	57	66	75	83	92	101	110	118	127	136	145	154	162	171	180	189	197	206
3.9	10	4	11	18	25	32	40	47	54	61	68	75	83	90	97	104	111	119	126	133	140	147	154	162	169
3.5	9	3	9	14	20	26	32	37	43	49	55	60	66	72	78	83	89	95	101	106	112	118	124	129	135
3.1	8	2	7	11	16	20	25	29	34	38	43	47	51	56	60	65	69	74	78	83	87	92	96	101	105
2.8	7	2	5	8	12	15	18	22	25	29	32	35	39	42	45	49	52	55	59	62	66	69	72	76	79
2.4	6	1	4	6	8	11	13	16	18	20	23	25	28	30	32	35	37	40	42	45	47	49	52	54	57
2.0	5	1	2	4	6	7	9	10	12	14	15	17	19	20	22	23	25	27	28	30	31	33	35	36	38
1.6	4	0	1	2	3	4	5	6	7	8	9	10	11	12	13	14	15	16	17	18	19	20	21	22	23
1.2	3	0	1	1	2	2	3	3	4	4	5	5	6	6	7	7	8	8	9	9	10	10	11	11	12
0.8	2	0	0	0	1	1	1	1	1	2	2	2	2	2	2	3	3	3	3	3	3	4	4	4	4
0	1	0	0	0	0	0	0	0	0	0	0	0	0	0	0	0	0	0	0	0	0	0	0	0	0
0	cm	1	2	3	4	5	6	7	8	9	10	11	12	13	14	15	16	17	18	19	20	21	22	23	24
Inches	0	0.4	0.8	1.2	1.6	2.0	2.4	2.8	3.1	3.5	3.9	4.3	4.7	5.1	5.5	5.9	6.3	6.7	7.1	7.5	7.9	8.3	8.7	9.1	9.4

Erect Penis Length (cm and inches)

There's a black line on the chart beginning between 9 and 10 cm in length and 20 cm in girth which moves down and to the left. The cells to the left of this line are the johnson dimensions in which a marginal increase in length would be *more* advantageous to penile volume than circumference. You can see it's a pretty small cluster of values, to which very few men fall within based on the distribution.

To give you a better sense of the prevalence of various 3D johnson sizes, the chart on the next page (Figure 22) displays the actual percentage values underlying the heat map.

Figure 22 – Erect Penis Size Distribution Matrix

Jacked Johnson

Erect Penis Size Matrix

Erect Penis Circumference (cm and inches)

7.9	20	0.0%	0.0%	0.0%	0.0%	0.0%	0.0%	0.0%	0.0%	0.0%	0.0%	0.0%	0.0%	0.0%	0.0%	0.0%	0.0%	0.0%	0.0%	0.0%	0.0%	0.0%	0.0%	0.0%	0.0%
7.5	19	0.0%	0.0%	0.0%	0.0%	0.0%	0.0%	0.0%	0.0%	0.0%	0.0%	0.0%	0.0%	0.0%	0.0%	0.0%	0.0%	0.0%	0.0%	0.0%	0.0%	0.0%	0.0%	0.0%	0.0%
7.1	18	0.0%	0.0%	0.0%	0.0%	0.0%	0.0%	0.0%	0.0%	0.0%	0.0%	0.0%	0.0%	0.0%	0.0%	0.0%	0.0%	0.0%	0.0%	0.0%	0.0%	0.0%	0.0%	0.0%	0.0%
6.7	17	0.0%	0.0%	0.0%	0.0%	0.0%	0.0%	0.0%	0.0%	0.0%	0.0%	0.0%	0.0%	0.0%	0.0%	0.0%	0.0%	0.0%	0.0%	0.0%	0.0%	0.0%	0.0%	0.0%	0.0%
6.3	16	0.0%	0.0%	0.0%	0.0%	0.0%	0.0%	0.0%	0.0%	0.0%	0.0%	0.1%	0.1%	0.1%	0.1%	0.1%	0.0%	0.0%	0.0%	0.0%	0.0%	0.0%	0.0%	0.0%	0.0%
5.9	15	0.0%	0.0%	0.0%	0.0%	0.0%	0.0%	0.0%	0.0%	0.1%	0.2%	0.4%	0.5%	0.6%	0.6%	0.4%	0.2%	0.1%	0.0%	0.0%	0.0%	0.0%	0.0%	0.0%	0.0%
5.5	14	0.0%	0.0%	0.0%	0.0%	0.0%	0.0%	0.0%	0.1%	0.3%	0.7%	1.4%	2.1%	2.4%	2.2%	1.5%	0.8%	0.3%	0.1%	0.0%	0.0%	0.0%	0.0%	0.0%	0.0%
5.1	13	0.0%	0.0%	0.0%	0.0%	0.0%	0.0%	0.0%	0.1%	0.6%	1.5%	2.9%	4.3%	5.0%	4.5%	3.0%	1.7%	0.7%	0.2%	0.1%	0.0%	0.0%	0.0%	0.0%	0.0%
4.7	12	0.0%	0.0%	0.0%	0.0%	0.0%	0.0%	0.1%	0.2%	0.8%	1.8%	3.6%	5.2%	6.1%	5.5%	3.7%	2.0%	0.8%	0.3%	0.1%	0.0%	0.0%	0.0%	0.0%	0.0%
4.3	11	0.0%	0.0%	0.0%	0.0%	0.0%	0.0%	0.0%	0.1%	0.5%	1.2%	2.4%	3.6%	4.2%	3.7%	2.5%	1.4%	0.5%	0.2%	0.0%	0.0%	0.0%	0.0%	0.0%	0.0%
3.9	10	0.0%	0.0%	0.0%	0.0%	0.0%	0.0%	0.0%	0.0%	0.2%	0.5%	0.9%	1.3%	1.5%	1.4%	0.9%	0.5%	0.2%	0.1%	0.0%	0.0%	0.0%	0.0%	0.0%	0.0%
3.5	9	0.0%	0.0%	0.0%	0.0%	0.0%	0.0%	0.0%	0.0%	0.0%	0.1%	0.2%	0.3%	0.3%	0.3%	0.2%	0.1%	0.0%	0.0%	0.0%	0.0%	0.0%	0.0%	0.0%	0.0%
3.1	8	0.0%	0.0%	0.0%	0.0%	0.0%	0.0%	0.0%	0.0%	0.0%	0.0%	0.0%	0.0%	0.0%	0.0%	0.0%	0.0%	0.0%	0.0%	0.0%	0.0%	0.0%	0.0%	0.0%	0.0%
2.8	7	0.0%	0.0%	0.0%	0.0%	0.0%	0.0%	0.0%	0.0%	0.0%	0.0%	0.0%	0.0%	0.0%	0.0%	0.0%	0.0%	0.0%	0.0%	0.0%	0.0%	0.0%	0.0%	0.0%	0.0%
2.4	6	0.0%	0.0%	0.0%	0.0%	0.0%	0.0%	0.0%	0.0%	0.0%	0.0%	0.0%	0.0%	0.0%	0.0%	0.0%	0.0%	0.0%	0.0%	0.0%	0.0%	0.0%	0.0%	0.0%	0.0%
2.0	5	0.0%	0.0%	0.0%	0.0%	0.0%	0.0%	0.0%	0.0%	0.0%	0.0%	0.0%	0.0%	0.0%	0.0%	0.0%	0.0%	0.0%	0.0%	0.0%	0.0%	0.0%	0.0%	0.0%	0.0%
1.6	4	0.0%	0.0%	0.0%	0.0%	0.0%	0.0%	0.0%	0.0%	0.0%	0.0%	0.0%	0.0%	0.0%	0.0%	0.0%	0.0%	0.0%	0.0%	0.0%	0.0%	0.0%	0.0%	0.0%	0.0%
1.2	3	0.0%	0.0%	0.0%	0.0%	0.0%	0.0%	0.0%	0.0%	0.0%	0.0%	0.0%	0.0%	0.0%	0.0%	0.0%	0.0%	0.0%	0.0%	0.0%	0.0%	0.0%	0.0%	0.0%	0.0%
0.8	2	0.0%	0.0%	0.0%	0.0%	0.0%	0.0%	0.0%	0.0%	0.0%	0.0%	0.0%	0.0%	0.0%	0.0%	0.0%	0.0%	0.0%	0.0%	0.0%	0.0%	0.0%	0.0%	0.0%	0.0%
0	1	0.0%	0.0%	0.0%	0.0%	0.0%	0.0%	0.0%	0.0%	0.0%	0.0%	0.0%	0.0%	0.0%	0.0%	0.0%	0.0%	0.0%	0.0%	0.0%	0.0%	0.0%	0.0%	0.0%	0.0%
0	cm	1	2	3	4	5	6	7	8	9	10	11	12	13	14	15	16	17	18	19	20	21	22	23	24
Inches	0	0.4	0.8	1.2	1.6	2.0	2.4	2.8	3.1	3.5	3.9	4.3	4.7	5.1	5.5	5.9	6.3	6.7	7.1	7.5	7.9	8.3	8.7	9.1	9.4

Erect Penis Length (cm and inches)

About 1 in 4 men are clustered within a tight range of 12.1 and 14.0 cm in length and between 11.1 cm and 13.0 cm in girth. Over half of men's johnsons are within a range of 11.1 cm and 15.0 cm in length and 10.1 cm and 13.0 cm in girth. If you go back to the first matrix chart (Figure 21), that's a volume range of 101 cc on the low end to 180 cc on the high end.

The final chart of this chapter is basically a multi-dimensional nomogram or cumulative distribution function. For a given erect johnson length and circumference, this chart displays the proportion of men that are smaller or the same size in terms of volume (Figure 23). It's like a 3D nomogram.

Jacked Johnson — **Erect Penis Size Matrix**

Erect Penis Circumference (cm and inches) / Erect Penis Length (cm and inches)

in	cm	1	2	3	4	5	6	7	8	9	10	11	12	13	14	15	16	17	18	19	20	21	22	23	24
7.5	19	0%	0%	1%	11%	37%	61%	82%	93%	98%	99%	100%	100%	100%	100%	100%	100%	100%	100%	100%	100%	100%	100%	100%	100%
7.1	18	0%	0%	1%	6%	23%	49%	72%	88%	94%	98%	99%	100%	100%	100%	100%	100%	100%	100%	100%	100%	100%	100%	100%	100%
6.7	17	0%	0%	0%	3%	13%	32%	51%	72%	88%	94%	98%	99%	100%	100%	100%	100%	100%	100%	100%	100%	100%	100%	100%	100%
6.3	16	0%	0%	0%	1%	6%	18%	37%	61%	72%	88%	93%	97%	98%	99%	100%	100%	100%	100%	100%	100%	100%	100%	100%	100%
5.9	15	0%	0%	0%	0%	2%	9%	19%	37%	57%	72%	82%	89%	95%	98%	99%	100%	100%	100%	100%	100%	100%	100%	100%	100%
5.5	14	0%	0%	0%	0%	1%	4%	11%	19%	37%	51%	62%	76%	88%	93%	96%	98%	99%	99%	100%	100%	100%	100%	100%	100%
5.1	13	0%	0%	0%	0%	0%	2%	4%	11%	19%	28%	42%	61%	72%	81%	86%	91%	94%	97%	98%	99%	99%	100%	100%	100%
4.7	12	0%	0%	0%	0%	0%	0%	2%	4%	7%	14%	26%	37%	49%	56%	66%	74%	82%	88%	91%	94%	96%	98%	98%	99%
4.3	11	0%	0%	0%	0%	0%	0%	0%	1%	2%	6%	11%	17%	23%	32%	40%	50%	61%	67%	72%	81%	82%	88%	93%	94%
3.9	10	0%	0%	0%	0%	0%	0%	0%	0%	1%	2%	3%	5%	9%	13%	18%	27%	32%	37%	49%	51%	61%	67%	72%	81%
3.5	9	0%	0%	0%	0%	0%	0%	0%	0%	0%	0%	1%	1%	2%	3%	6%	6%	11%	14%	19%	27%	27%	37%	40%	49%
3.1	8	0%	0%	0%	0%	0%	0%	0%	0%	0%	0%	0%	0%	0%	1%	1%	2%	2%	3%	5%	6%	9%	11%	14%	18%
2.8	7	0%	0%	0%	0%	0%	0%	0%	0%	0%	0%	0%	0%	0%	0%	0%	0%	0%	0%	1%	1%	2%	2%	3%	4%
2.4	6	0%	0%	0%	0%	0%	0%	0%	0%	0%	0%	0%	0%	0%	0%	0%	0%	0%	0%	0%	0%	0%	0%	0%	0%
2.0	5	0%	0%	0%	0%	0%	0%	0%	0%	0%	0%	0%	0%	0%	0%	0%	0%	0%	0%	0%	0%	0%	0%	0%	0%
1.6	4	0%	0%	0%	0%	0%	0%	0%	0%	0%	0%	0%	0%	0%	0%	0%	0%	0%	0%	0%	0%	0%	0%	0%	0%
1.2	3	0%	0%	0%	0%	0%	0%	0%	0%	0%	0%	0%	0%	0%	0%	0%	0%	0%	0%	0%	0%	0%	0%	0%	0%
0.8	2	0%	0%	0%	0%	0%	0%	0%	0%	0%	0%	0%	0%	0%	0%	0%	0%	0%	0%	0%	0%	0%	0%	0%	0%
0.4	1	0%	0%	0%	0%	0%	0%	0%	0%	0%	0%	0%	0%	0%	0%	0%	0%	0%	0%	0%	0%	0%	0%	0%	0%
0	cm	1	2	3	4	5	6	7	8	9	10	11	12	13	14	15	16	17	18	19	20	21	22	23	24
Inches	0	0.4	0.8	1.2	1.6	2.0	2.4	2.8	3.1	3.5	3.9	4.3	4.7	5.1	5.5	5.9	6.3	6.7	7.1	7.5	7.9	8.3	8.7	9.1	9.4

Erect Penis Length (cm and inches)

Part III: The Flaccid Johnson

The Protean Penis: Flaccid Length

In my humble opinion, the flaccid penis is the funniest thing in the human anatomy. It's essentially useless, except its tube-like design allows a man to control the direction of his urine; a key feature that gives him the luxury of peeing standing up. Besides, the not-having-to-squat-to-pee thing (which I love by the way), the flaccid johnson is usually just getting in the way. I mean a man can't use it for sex, you can't see it through clothing, and it's always getting pinched, pulled and stuck to his leg. I've been told by guys with woolly mammoth trunk sized flaccid johnsons that they have difficulty buying comfortable underwear and have to adjust themselves constantly. These men also have a much larger target for hilarious but debilitating pain when playing sports or because of sophomoric pranks. Oh, it just sounds awful! Thank god I'm not plagued with that aggravation.

A few years ago, I never would've considered performing an analysis on male flaccid johnson size. I assumed it didn't really concern men and that only erect size mattered. I mean, unless a man has desires to be a nude model, a professional streaker, or an actor who does full frontal nude scenes like Michael Fassbender (#legend), what's with all the anxiety and concern over something that's essentially a decoration? Give me an ugly flaccid but beautiful erect penis every day of the week. The johnson's two states remind me of a famous golf saying: "drive for show, putt for dough", except for the johnson it's: "flaccid for show, erect for dough"; or erect for mo'…as in getting mo' sex! If you don't like sports, it's like a beautiful Hollywood starlet who looks terrible without makeup. As long as she looks terrific when the cameras are rolling, she'll keep getting a lot of work and notoriety, just like a johnson.

Well, it turns out that flaccid johnson size matters to men…a lot! A 2005 study published in the Electronic Journal of Human Sexuality surveyed

Canadian post-secondary students about their satisfaction with the appearance and size of their penis in the erect and flaccid states (Morrison et al, 2005). The results showed that males were five times more dissatisfied with the length and appearance of their flaccid penis compared to their erect penis; five times!

A 2002 study (Mondaini et al, 2002) published in the Journal of Impotence Research showed that two thirds of men that had sought out penile enlargement surgery were looking to improve their flaccid size only! You read that right; only flaccid, and not erect size.

I can't deny those numbers. The next several chapters will follow the same sequence as the erect johnson. Flaccid johnson size data was a lot easier to find since that's the johnson's natural state and the difficulty and awkwardness of conjuring up an erection in front of a dude in rubber gloves is removed.

Five studies made the cut to build a robust distribution for flaccid length totalling over 5,000 men from all over the globe. The chosen studies are summarized in Figure 24.

Study	Country	Sample Size	Age	Mean	S.D.	Min	Max
Wessells et al. (1996)	USA	80	54	8.9	2.4	5.0	15.5
Aslan et al. (2011)	Turkey	1152	20	9.3	1.3	5.7	14.0
Ponchietti et al. (2001)	Italy	3300	18	9.0	2.0	4.0	12.5
Promodu et al. (2007)	India	301	32	8.2	1.4	4.5	13.0
Park et al. (1998)	Korea	309	41	7.8	1.2	4.5	12.5
Summary (cm)		5142	33	8.6	1.6	4.0	15.5
Summary (inches)		5142	33	3.4	0.6	1.6	6.1

Three of the studies should look familiar as they were included in the erect johnson size analysis. The two new joiners followed the same methodology I outlined earlier in the book. They also have massive sample sizes, with the Italian study having the largest number of participants ever recorded in a penis size study. Oddly enough, both new studies procured their large numbers of participants from the military; yet another reason to appreciate our brave men in uniform.

It was especially important to find studies with larger sample sizes for the flaccid johnson because of its notoriously mercurial nature. I mean, my flaccid johnson will take on about a hundred different shapes and sizes throughout the day. If it was a person, it would've been institutionalized years ago. Relatively speaking, it ranges from a lanky and confident serpent-like shape to a terrified turtlehead. Imagine if some of your limbs were that fickle? If your arms and legs changed size whenever they wanted? How would you buy clothes?

Anyways, Figure 25 is a histogram of the distribution created from the studies. All five studies were weighted equally.

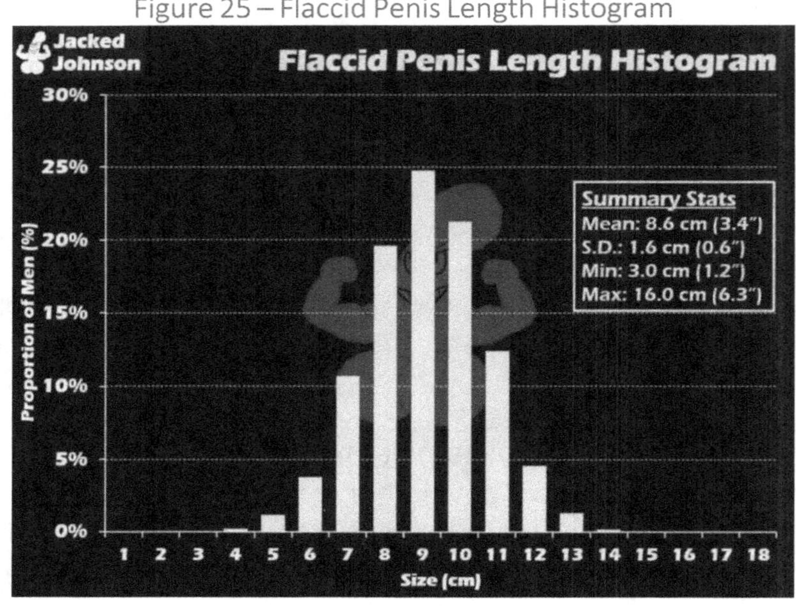

The average flaccid johnson length is 8.6 cm (3.4"), which is about the length of a man's index finger or his credit card. There's a massive chasm between the shortest and longest johnsons, with the shortest coming in at 3 cm (1.2") and the longest 16.0 cm (6.3"). Drop the temperature enough, and that widely dispersed histogram becomes a single bar centred around 3 cm very quickly. Shrinkage is not a myth!

All studies included in the distribution carefully controlled for temperature, which should quell any shrinkage concerns you might have.

8 We're all the same: Flaccid Circumference

Four of the five studies used for building the flaccid length distribution were also used for flaccid circumference. Unfortunately, one of the larger studies (Aslan et al.) did not measure flaccid circumference but I've managed to swap in a rock solid study published in 2002 based out of Greece. So once again, we have five equally weighted studies from disparate parts of the globe making up the distribution. The studies are summarized in Figure 26.

Flaccid Penis Circumference - Summary of Studies Used							
Study	Country	Sample Size	Age	Mean	S.D.	Min	Max
Wessells et al. (1996)	USA	80	54	9.7	1.2	6.5	13.0
Spyropoulos et al. (2002)	Greece	52	26	8.7	1.1	6.0	11.0
Ponchietti et al. (2001)	Italy	3300	18	10.0	0.8	8.0	12.0
Promodu et al. (2007)	India	301	32	9.1	1.0	6.0	12.5
Park et al. (1998)	Korea	309	41	9.0	1.2	8.0	13.5
Summary (cm)		4042	34	9.3	1.0	6.0	13.5
Summary (inches)		4042	34	3.7	0.4	2.4	5.3

The average circumference value of 9.3 cm means that the average flaccid johnson is wider than it is long. Recall that the average flaccid length is 8.6 cm (3.4"). The variability of flaccid circumference is quite low (standard deviation is only 1 cm), which means two-thirds of guys are less than an inch apart. Figure 27 is a histogram of the distribution.

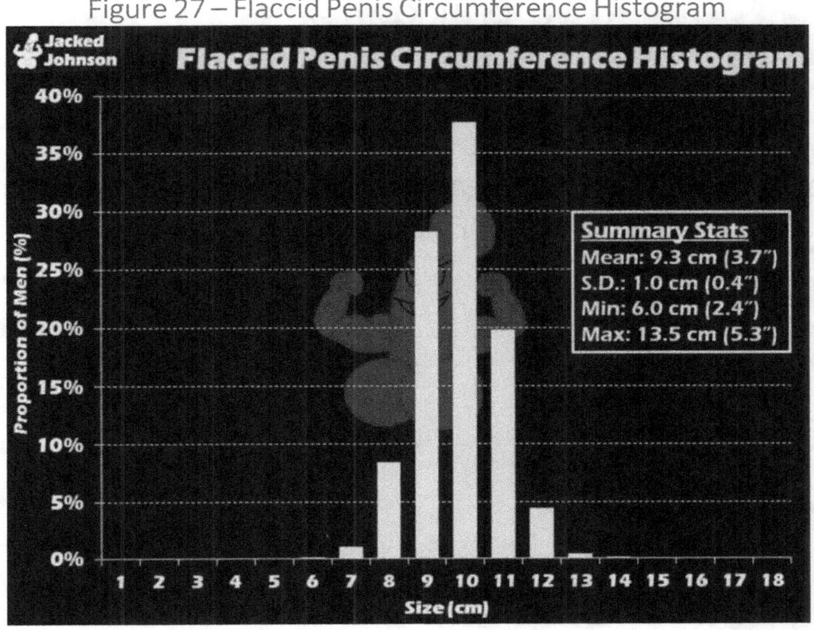

Even the range of values at the extremes is narrow for flaccid width, with the narrowest flaccid johnson measuring 6 cm (2.4") and the widest 13.5 cm (5.3").

Based on this distribution, any man achieving locker room notoriety related to his johnson size won't be getting it because of his girth.

9 Fully Flaccid

If the average flaccid johnson was a person, it would be morbidly obese. To give you a better feel for its dimensions, I've created another comparison chart of similarly sized objects in Figure 28.

Jacked Johnson	**Is that a roll of quarters in your pocket?** Flaccid Penis Size Comparisons				
Object	Length (cm)	Circumference (cm)	Length Difference (absolute)	Width Difference (absolute)	Total Difference (cm)
Flaccid Penis	8.6	9.3	-	-	-
Roll of Toonies ($2 CAD Coin)	4.5	8.8	4.1	0.5	4.6
Roll of US Quarters	7.3	7.6	1.3	1.7	3.0
Credit Card	8.4	5.0	0.3	4.3	4.6
Playing Card	8.5	4.5	0.1	4.8	4.9
Male Index Finger	8.6	8.2	0.0	1.1	1.1
Beer Bottle Label (335mL)	8.8	19.1	0.2	9.8	10.0
Wine Cork	4.5	7.3	4.1	2.0	6.1

It turns out that the average flaccid johnson is identical in length to an average male index finger; how about that? Playing cards, a credit card, and a beer bottle label are also very close. In terms of circumference, I'm proud to say a toonie, the two dollar coin from my native Canada, is closest. I'm not sure if a penis is what the Canadian mint based the size of the toonie on, but it's fair to speculate. The Euro two dollar coin also has some girth (about 8.1 cm in circumference), but not quite as much as we Canadians. Across all dimensions, an average index finger is very close, followed by a roll of US quarters.

Despite average flaccid johnson width and length being almost identical, their respective distributions are quite different. Ironically, the distribution of flaccid penis *length* is much shorter and wider than the distribution of flaccid penis *width*. The variability of flaccid length is actually *twice* that of flaccid width on a relative basis. In fact, flaccid length has the most variability of any flaccid or erect penile dimension. This could help explain men's higher anxiety and dissatisfaction about the size of their flaccid johnson compared to their erect johnson. If men's heights were as varied as their flaccid penis lengths, one out of five men would be considered dwarfs, while one in ten would be over seven feet tall! A histogram of flaccid length and circumference is presented in Figure 29.

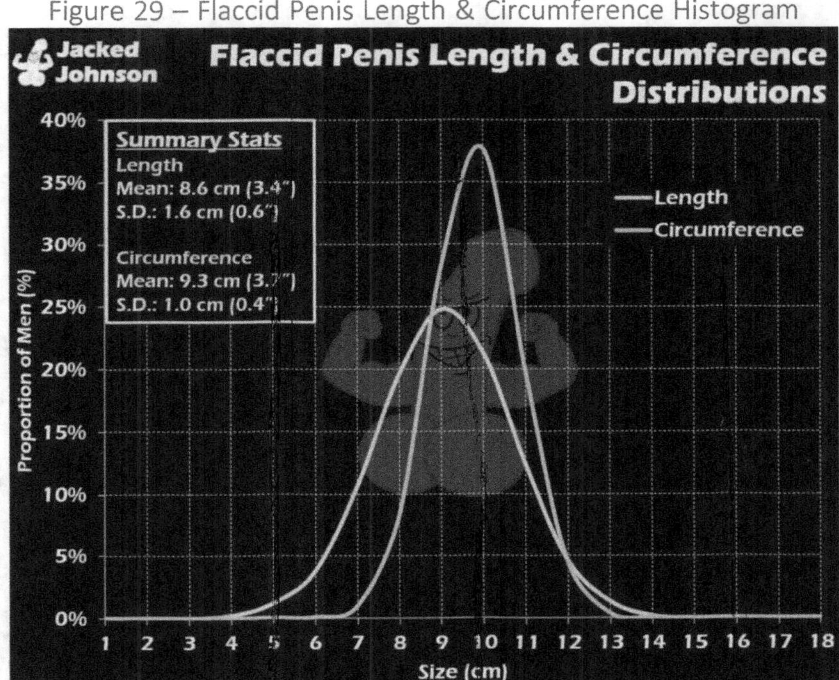

Although they're barely half a centimeter apart in terms of average, the stark difference in variability for circumference and length is evident in the graph. The long and narrow bell curve of flaccid circumference is the Luigi to the short and stalky bell curve of flaccid length's Mario. A nomogram of flaccid Johnson length and circumference is shown in Figure 30.

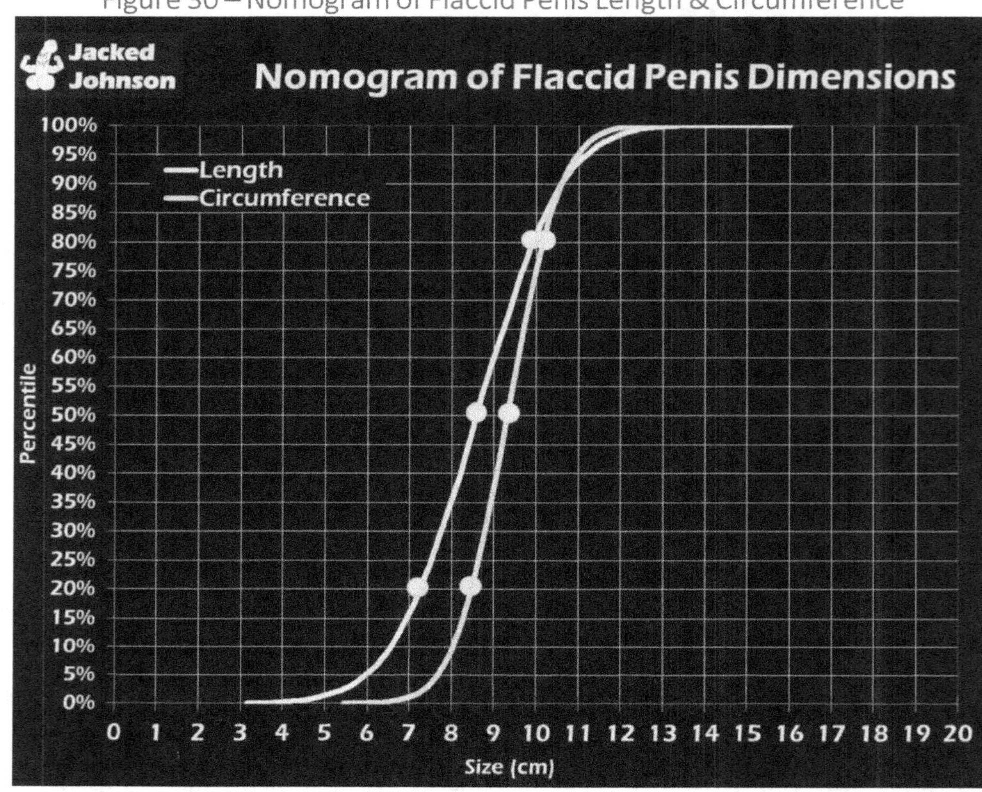

The width line is much steeper in comparison to the length line. A steeper line means that a larger proportion of men are separated by a narrower range of values.

Four out of five men have a flaccid length between 6.7 cm (2.6") and 11 cm (4.3") and are separated by 4.3 cm (1.7"). The middle half of men range from 7.5 cm (3") to 9.9 cm (3.9"), which separates them by less than 2.4 cm (0.9") in length.

In terms of width, four out of five men measure between 8.1 cm (3.2") and 10.7 cm (4.2"). Half of men are separated by less than 1.4 cm (0.55"), which is barely distinguishable to the naked eye when you're naked. A chart to aid in the interpretation of the nomogram is shown in Figure 31.

Jacked Johnson	Flaccid Penis Dimensions by Percentile		
Percentile	Explanation	Length	Circumference
10%	Bigger than or equal to 1 out of 10 guys	6.5 cm	7.9 cm
20%	Bigger than or equal to 1 out of 5 guys	7.3 cm	8.3 cm
30%	Bigger than or equal to 3 out of 10 guys	7.8 cm	8.7 cm
40%	Bigger than or equal to 2 out of 5 guys	8.2 cm	8.9 cm
50%	Bigger than or equal to 1 out of 2 guys	8.6 cm	9.2 cm
60%	Bigger than or equal to 3 out of 5 guys	9.1 cm	9.5 cm
70%	Bigger than or equal to 7 out of 10 guys	9.5 cm	9.7 cm
80%	Bigger than or equal to 4 out of 5 guys	10.0 cm	10.0 cm
90%	Bigger than or equal to 9 out of 10 guys	10.7 cm	10.5 cm
99%	Bigger than or equal to 99 out of 100 guys	12.4 cm	11.6 cm

Figure 32 is a chart that displays flaccid volume for a given length and circumference. A heat map is overlaid on top which is representative of the proportion of men's johnsons falling within those values.

Flaccid Penis Volume by Circumference and Length

volume measured in cm^3 (cc)

Jacked Johnson

Flaccid Penis Circumference (cm and inches)

inches	cm	1	2	3	4	5	6	7	8	9	10	11	12	13	14	15	16	17	18	19	20
7.9	20	15	45	76	106	136	166	197	227	257	287	318	348	378	409	439	469	499	530	560	590
7.5	19	14	41	68	95	123	150	177	204	232	259	286	313	340	368	395	422	449	477	504	531
7.1	18	12	37	61	85	110	134	158	183	207	232	256	280	305	329	353	378	402	426	451	475
6.7	17	11	32	54	76	97	119	141	162	184	206	227	249	271	292	314	336	357	379	401	422
6.3	16	10	29	48	67	86	105	124	143	163	182	201	220	239	258	277	296	315	335	354	373
5.9	15	8	25	42	59	75	92	109	125	142	159	176	192	209	226	243	259	276	293	310	326
5.5	14	7	22	36	51	65	80	94	109	123	138	152	167	181	196	210	225	239	254	268	283
5.1	13	6	19	31	44	56	68	81	93	106	118	131	143	155	168	180	193	205	218	230	242
4.7	12	5	16	26	37	47	58	68	79	89	100	111	121	132	142	153	163	174	184	195	205
4.3	11	4	13	22	31	39	48	57	66	75	83	92	101	110	118	127	136	145	154	162	171
3.9	10	4	11	18	25	32	40	47	54	61	68	75	83	90	97	104	111	119	126	133	140
3.5	9	3	9	14	20	26	32	37	43	49	55	60	66	72	78	83	89	95	101	106	112
3.1	8	2	7	11	16	20	25	29	34	38	43	47	51	56	60	65	69	74	78	83	87
2.8	7	2	5	8	12	15	18	22	25	29	32	35	39	42	45	49	52	55	59	62	66
2.4	6	1	4	6	8	11	13	16	18	20	23	25	28	30	32	35	37	40	42	45	47
2.0	5	1	2	4	6	7	9	10	12	14	15	17	19	20	22	23	25	27	28	30	31
1.6	4	0	1	2	3	4	5	6	7	8	9	10	11	12	13	14	15	16	17	18	19
1.2	3	0	1	1	2	2	3	3	4	4	5	5	6	6	7	7	8	8	9	9	10
0.8	2	0	0	0	1	1	1	1	1	2	2	2	2	2	2	3	3	3	3	3	3
0	1	0	0	0	0	0	0	0	0	0	0	0	0	0	0	0	0	0	0	0	0
0	cm	1	2	3	4	5	6	7	8	9	10	11	12	13	14	15	16	17	18	19	20
inches	0	0.4	0.8	1.2	1.6	2.0	2.4	2.8	3.1	3.5	3.9	4.3	4.7	5.1	5.5	5.9	6.3	6.7	7.1	7.5	7.9

Flaccid Penis Length (cm and inches)

Figure 33 is the same chart as <u>Figure 32</u> with the proporion values listed. Each number represents the approximate proporion of men falling within a given johnson size range.

Figure 33 – Flaccid Penis Size Distribution Matrix Chart

Jacked Johnson

Flaccid Penis Size Matrix

Flaccid Penis Circumference (cm and inches)

6.3	16	0.0%	0.0%	0.0%	0.0%	0.0%	0.0%	0.0%	0.0%	0.0%	0.0%	0.0%	0.0%	0.0%	0.0%	0.0%	0.0%
5.9	15	0.0%	0.0%	0.0%	0.0%	0.0%	0.0%	0.0%	0.0%	0.0%	0.0%	0.0%	0.0%	0.0%	0.0%	0.0%	0.0%
5.5	14	0.0%	0.0%	0.0%	0.0%	0.0%	0.0%	0.0%	0.0%	0.0%	0.0%	0.0%	0.0%	0.0%	0.0%	0.0%	0.0%
5.1	13	0.0%	0.0%	0.0%	0.0%	0.0%	0.0%	0.0%	0.1%	0.1%	0.1%	0.0%	0.0%	0.0%	0.0%	0.0%	0.0%
4.7	12	0.0%	0.0%	0.0%	0.0%	0.1%	0.2%	0.5%	0.9%	1.1%	0.9%	0.5%	0.2%	0.1%	0.0%	0.0%	0.0%
4.3	11	0.0%	0.0%	0.0%	0.0%	0.2%	0.7%	2.1%	3.9%	4.9%	4.2%	2.5%	0.9%	0.3%	0.0%	0.0%	0.0%
3.9	10	0.0%	0.0%	0.0%	0.1%	0.4%	1.4%	4.0%	7.4%	9.3%	8.0%	4.7%	1.7%	0.5%	0.1%	0.0%	0.0%
3.5	9	0.0%	0.0%	0.0%	0.1%	0.3%	1.1%	3.0%	5.5%	7.0%	6.0%	3.5%	1.3%	0.4%	0.1%	0.0%	0.0%
3.1	8	0.0%	0.0%	0.0%	0.0%	0.1%	0.3%	0.9%	1.6%	2.1%	1.8%	1.0%	0.4%	0.1%	0.0%	0.0%	0.0%
2.8	7	0.0%	0.0%	0.0%	0.0%	0.0%	0.0%	0.1%	0.2%	0.2%	0.2%	0.1%	0.0%	0.0%	0.0%	0.0%	0.0%
2.4	6	0.0%	0.0%	0.0%	0.0%	0.0%	0.0%	0.0%	0.0%	0.0%	0.0%	0.0%	0.0%	0.0%	0.0%	0.0%	0.0%
2.0	5	0.0%	0.0%	0.0%	0.0%	0.0%	0.0%	0.0%	0.0%	0.0%	0.0%	0.0%	0.0%	0.0%	0.0%	0.0%	0.0%
1.6	4	0.0%	0.0%	0.0%	0.0%	0.0%	0.0%	0.0%	0.0%	0.0%	0.0%	0.0%	0.0%	0.0%	0.0%	0.0%	0.0%
1.2	3	0.0%	0.0%	0.0%	0.0%	0.0%	0.0%	0.0%	0.0%	0.0%	0.0%	0.0%	0.0%	0.0%	0.0%	0.0%	0.0%
0.8	2	0.0%	0.0%	0.0%	0.0%	0.0%	0.0%	0.0%	0.0%	0.0%	0.0%	0.0%	0.0%	0.0%	0.0%	0.0%	0.0%
0.4	1	0.0%	0.0%	0.0%	0.0%	0.0%	0.0%	0.0%	0.0%	0.0%	0.0%	0.0%	0.0%	0.0%	0.0%	0.0%	0.0%
	cm	1	2	3	4	5	6	7	8	9	10	11	12	13	14	15	16
Inches		0.4	0.8	1.2	1.6	2.0	2.4	2.8	3.1	3.5	3.9	4.3	4.7	5.1	5.5	5.9	6.3

Flaccid Penis Length (cm and inches)

Part IV: Johnson Growth

10

Dr. Johnson and Mr. Jacked

So far in this book, we've analyzed the flaccid and erect johnsons separately but as we know they are effectively two versions of the same person...and one of them is a jacked up maniac! Like Dr. Jekyll and Mr. Hyde, or Dr. Bruce Banner and the Hulk. You just can't have one without the other.

To help visualize the johnson's transformation, Figure 34 is a histogram of the flaccid and erect length distributions. The associated nomogram is shown in Figure 35.

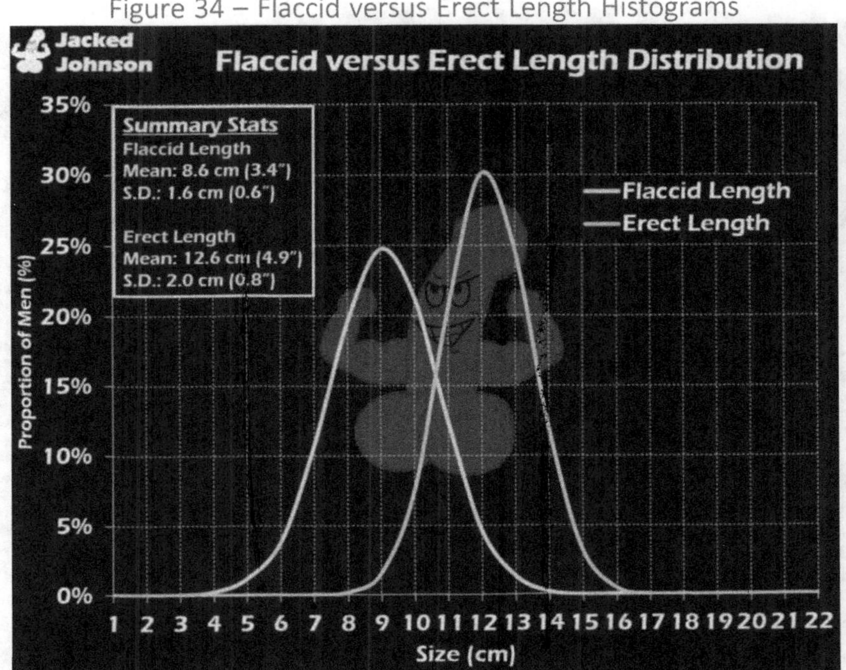
Jacked Johnson
Flaccid versus Erect Length Distribution
Summary Stats
Flaccid Length
Mean: 8.6 cm (3.4")
S.D.: 1.6 cm (0.6")
Erect Length
Mean: 12.6 cm (4.9")
S.D.: 2.0 cm (0.8")
Flaccid Length
Erect Length
35%
30%
25%
20%
15%
10%
5%
0%
Proportion of Men (%)
1 2 3 4 5 6 7 8 9 10 11 12 13 14 15 16 17 18 19 20 21 22
Size (cm)

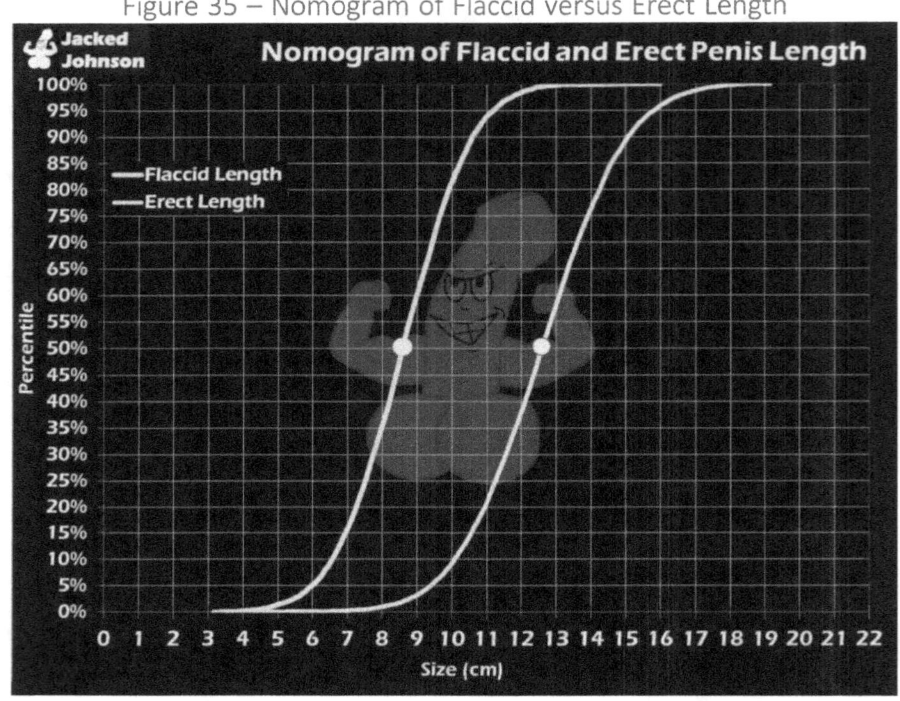

The average flaccid Johnson is almost exactly *two-thirds* the length of the average erect johnson. This means the typical Johnson grows about 4 cm (1.6") or 50 percent in length from flaccid to erect. The relative variability of flaccid lengths is much wider than erect (18.4% to 15.6%), which like I mentioned earlier, could explain men's higher flaccid anxiety. Fortunately, the inherent waywardness of the flaccid johnson appears to moderate when everyone's erect.

The johnson transformation in terms of circumference is not nearly as dramatic or volatile as length. When compared to its erect size, the average flaccid johnson increases about 2.4 cm (0.9") in circumference or 25 percent. The relative variability of flaccid and erect circumference is almost identical. The histograms are shown in Figure 36.

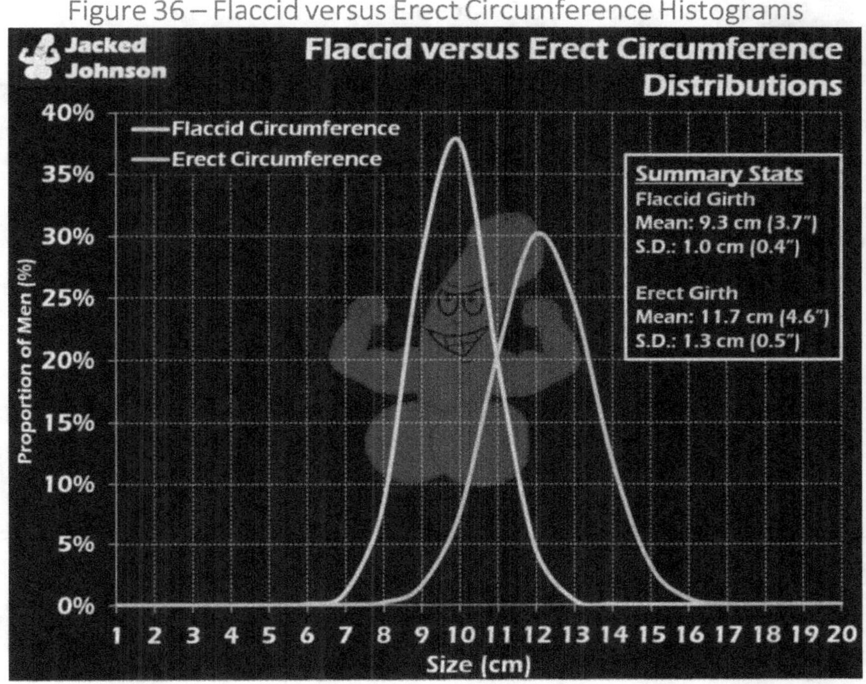

The key johnson measurements from the derived distributions across both states are summarized in Figure 37.

Figure 37 – Flaccid to Erect Penis Growth Summary Chart

The Four Key Johnson Dimensions
Jacked Johnson Model

Measurement	Flaccid Mean (S.D.)	Erect Mean (S.D.)	Difference in cm	Difference in %	Relative Var Flaccid	Relative Var Erect
Length	8.6 (1.6)	12.6 (2.0)	4.0	47%	19%	16%
Circumference	9.3 (1.0)	11.7 (1.3)	2.4	26%	11%	11%
Volume	59	137	78	131%		

In terms of volume, the average flaccid Johnson grows from an average of about 59 cc to 137 cc, an increase of 78 cc or 131 percent. A 3D diagram drawn to approximate scale is shown in Figure 38. The dimensions displayed in the diagram are length and diameter. Johnson diameter represents its linear width and can be derived from circumference.

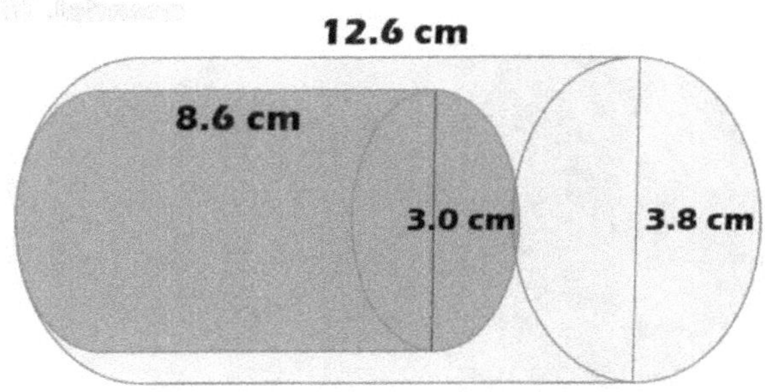

The four johnson size distributions created for this book are rock solid, and the theory used to analyze johnson growth is sound, but I would be remiss in my role as johnson size expert if I didn't take it a step further. See, you can take the numbers I've presented to you so far to the bank. You can print out life sized scale photos of my charts, lay your Johnson across them, and be confident you're giving yourself a fair shake. But in terms of johnson growth specifically, we need to dig deeper.

To ensure I have truly robust johnson growth analysis, I need to measure the same johnsons. No, not me personally! In other words, I need to *observe* data from the same group of johnsons in both the flaccid and erect states, rather than taking the mean difference between two aggregated distributions.

For that, we turn to an assemblage of studies published over the last several decades which analyzed johnson growth from the flaccid to erect state. There are a few new studies on the list. The new studies are able to be included because their methods are sound and now I'm indifferent to measurement method (i.e. bone pressed or non-bone pressed) because I'm only interested in the *relative* size change. As long as the researchers measured the johnson from the same location on each guy in the flaccid and erect states, we're good to go. A summary of the studies utilized for johnson length growth is presented in Figure 39.

Jacked Johnson	Summary of Studies Measuring Flaccid and Erect Penis Length				
Study	Average Age	Flaccid Length	Erect Length	Flaccid to Erect Growth	Flaccid to Erect Growth
Mehraban et al. (2006)	30	8.2	12.9	4.7	57%
Wessells et al. (1996)	54	8.9	12.3	3.4	39%
Awwad et al. (2004)	45	7.7	11.8	4.1	53%
Promodu et al. (2007)	32	8.2	13.0	4.8	58%
Park et al. (1998)	42	7.8	11.9	4.1	53%
Summary (cm)	41	8.1	12.4	4.2	52%
Summary (inches)	41	3.2	4.9	1.7	52%

The results from the five studies validate my data. The average johnson will grow roughly 50 percent in length from flaccid to erect. The average absolute growth of 4.2 cm or 1.7 inches obtained from these studies is also very close to the 4.0 cm (1.6") growth I calculated.

Four studies passed my smell test that analyzed johnson circumference growth from the flaccid to erect states. The results are summarized in Figure 40.

Jacked Johnson	Summary of Studies Measuring Flaccid and Erect Penis Circumference				
Study	Mean Age	Flaccid Circumference (cm)	Erect Circumference (cm)	Flaccid to Erect Incr (cm)	Flaccid to Erect Incr (%)
Mehraban et al. (2006)	30	9.1	11.5	2.3	25%
Wessells et al. (1996)	54	9.7	12.3	2.6	27%
Yoon et al. (1998)	22	8.3	11.2	2.8	34%
Park et al. (1998)	42	9.0	12.1	3.1	34%
Summary (cm)	37	9.1	11.8	2.7	30%
Summary (inches)	37	3.6	4.6	1.1	30%

Once again, my earlier calculation comes in pretty close. The average percentage increase in johnson circumference across the four studies was 30 percent, slightly above the 26 percent calculated from my distributions. Absolute growth averaged 2.7 cm (1.1"), compared to my calculation of 2.4 cm (0.9").

The Aging Johnson

The results *between* studies that analyzed johnson growth don't have a lot of variation, but if you look closely, an alarming trend emerges. Notice in the length chart (Figure 39) how the lowest growth figures appear in the study with the oldest group of participants (Wessells et al). The opposite is also true; the best growth figures appear in the studies with the youngest participants (Mehraban et al. and Promodu et al.). When the five studies' results are plotted in a graph, the terrifying trend becomes all the more real. The graphs are shown in Figure 41.

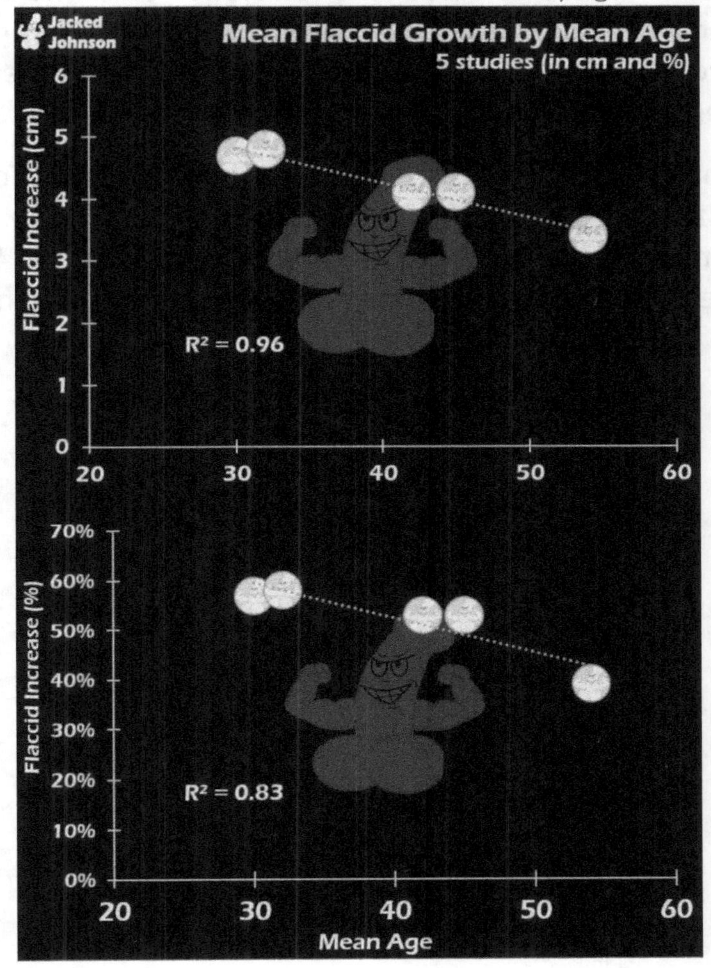

Whether measured in absolute (cm) or relative (%) terms, johnson growth displays a pretty strong negative relationship with age.

Intuitively, it makes some sense that a man could lose some length off his fastball as he gets older. The erect penis relies on adequate blood flow and the stretchiness of key components. Both of these attributes get impaired all over a man's body as he ages!

A preponderance of studies have run a correlation of johnson length versus age but the results have been mixed. This is definitely good news but that approach isn't ideal. Some compelling evidence has emerged in research when johnson growth is isolated and analyzed separately.

Two now familiar studies performed a more thorough statistical analysis on johnson size versus age, including flaccid to erect increase. A formal statistical comparison of participants younger and older than 40 years old was performed by both studies. The results are summarized in Figure 42.

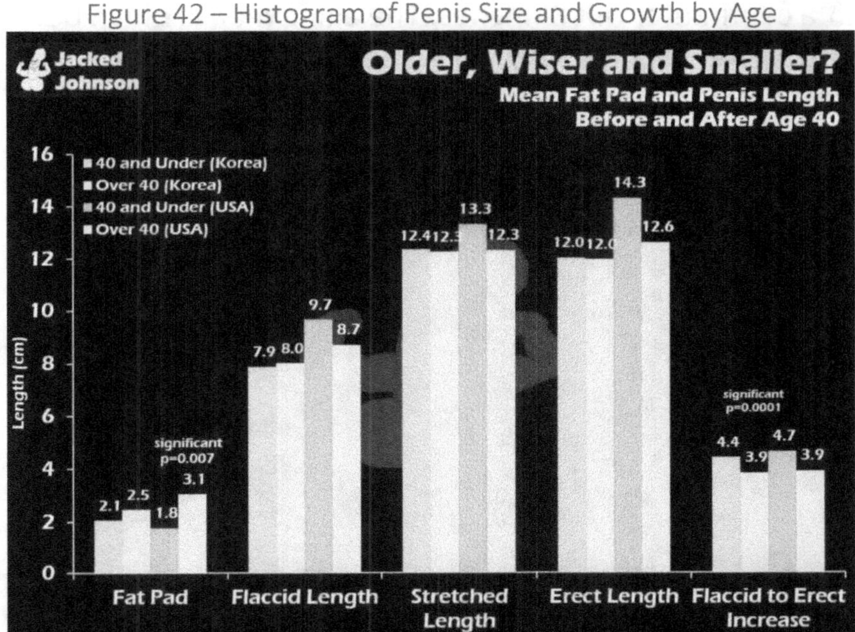

Both studies showed less flaccid to erect growth for men over 40 compared to men under 40 (far right of the graph). The results were statistically significant for the Park et al. study from Korea but not for the Wessells et al. The Wessells et al. study actually showed a larger difference in johnson growth but was stymied by its small sample size as compared to Park (80 men versus 300). Smaller sample sizes make it more difficult to prove differences didn't occur by random chance. Like I mention in the Glossary of Terms, statistical tests are analogous to presenting evidence in a court case. If you have fewer articles of evidence to show the jury (i.e. smaller sample size), then what you do present has to be really compelling.

Overall, the shrinking johnson case as a man ages is far from open and shut. I'd like to see it studied more in depth and broken out into more age groups instead of the binary categorization of above and below 40 years old. Even if we accept the Park et al. results as fact, it's only a decrease of about half a centimeter or 0.2 inches. The aging man is much better off worrying about keeping his swelling waistline at bay!

11

The Legends of Growers and Show-ers

The human body loves proportionality. When a jacked guy at the gym does a bicep curl, his already outsized bicep muscle fills with blood and becomes even larger, at least temporarily. A scrawny guy with arms like bamboo sticks looks slightly less scrawny when performing the same exercise; he doesn't suddenly turn into Lou Ferrigno (I've added his Wikipedia page link so that anyone under 40 can look him up…I'll wait).

The same proportionality is observed with women's breasts. When a large breasted woman gets aroused, her already ginormous melons will swell up and become temporarily larger. A small chested woman…OK, I know you get the idea…a Kate Hudson isn't going to swell into a Kate Upton in front of your eyes! That's just how the human body works. What you see is what you get. Everything follows a predictable linear path. Why would a penis be any different?

But perhaps you've heard stories; tales from ancient folklore; of proud men held in the highest of esteem among their peers. But in reality, these men are fakes, nothing but lowly charlatans! These men are not who they portray themselves to be; like a car with a Ferrari body but a pinto engine under the hood. Men who have the penile equivalent of a big budget summer movie with a story that never gets off the ground. These men have come to be known as "Show-ers."

Perhaps you've also heard legends of great men; men who are skilled alchemists; men who pull off the penile equivalent of transforming water into wine. These men are not seeped in style but rich in substance. Although it's easy to dismiss these men when glancing in their direction at a urinal or showering at the gym, they will make you rue the day you ever marginalized them. These men have come to be known as "Growers."

I know what you're thinking: these outlandish claims can't possibly be true. Just another cock-and-bull story, the stuff of fables! I know I thought the same thing as my father regaled me with legends of Growers and Show-ers as a boy. I assumed he was only trying to assuage my torment from Grade 9 Gym class. But as they say, sometimes a theory is so crazy, it's crazy enough to be true.

To investigate these mythical characters, we'll consult our old friends the Wessells et al. and Park et al. studies. Both studies plotted the individual johnson measurements of their participants. Figure 43 is a scatter plot of each participant's flaccid length against their erect length. Both studies' johnsons are shown in the same graph and colour coded.

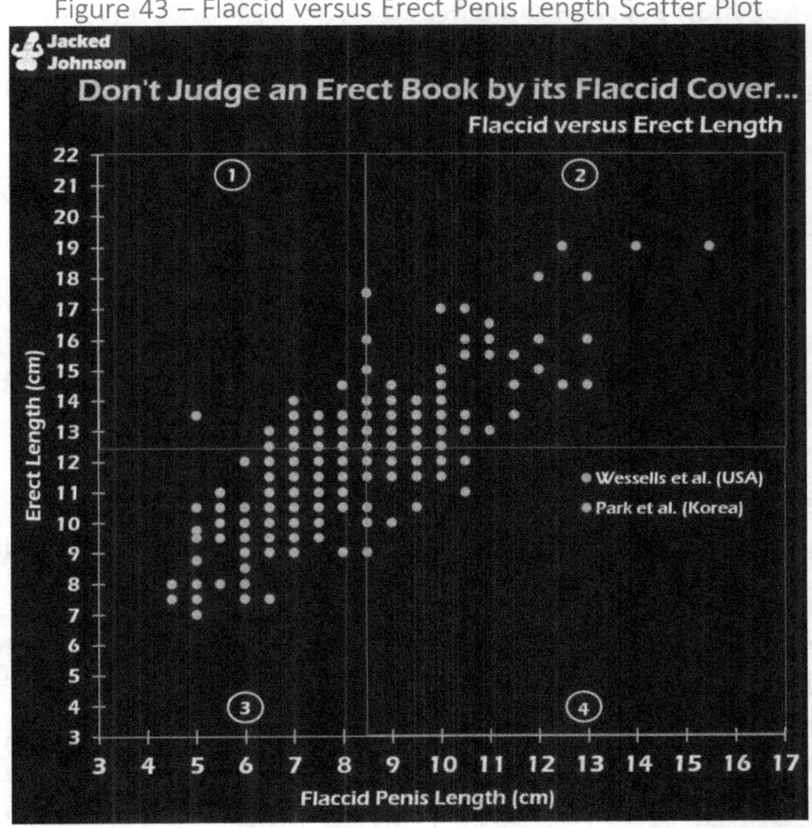

You can see a pretty decent linear relationship between flaccid and erect length. This is supported by coefficient of determination (R-squared) values of 0.68 and 0.59 for the Wessells et al. and Park et al. studies respectively. However, 0.68 is far from 1.0. There's still a lot of variation in erect lengths for a given flaccid length.

Take the 8.5 cm flaccid length values for example; that's roughly the average flaccid johnson length. Corresponding erect lengths for an 8.5 cm flaccid johnson are as short as 9 cm to as long as 17.5 cm. This means the same flaccid penis might double in size or barely grow at all!

Put another way, the inherent uncertainty of johnson growth means that an average flaccid johnson can become 4 cm (1.6") shorter or as much as 5 cm (2") larger than average once erect. A flaccid johnson is akin to Forrest Gump's box of chocolates metaphor about life: you just don't know what you're gonna get!

Before getting too carried away, looking again at the graph, the strength of the linear relationship does tell you that there are limits to my 'box of chocolates' penis notion.

To better illustrate this, I drew four quadrants in Figure 43. All dots in quadrants 1 and 3, or to the left of the line that runs vertically from 8.6 cm (the average flaccid length), are *below* average sized *flaccid* johnsons in terms of length. Of these same points (below average flaccid length johnsons), the ones located in quadrant 1 are the ones that grow into *above* average length *erect* johnsons. Despite the flaccid johnson's high growth variability, it's pretty evident that a guy hung like a mosquito won't grow into Ron Jeremy...even after foreplay from a couple of Ron's co-stars!

On the flip side, quadrants 2 and 4 have *above* average *flaccid* johnson lengths. Quadrant 2 values display the johnsons that remained above average in the erect state. Quadrant 4 are your extreme 'show-ers' and despite a significant head start, end up falling behind the average at the erect finish line. Despite its smaller populace, I always assume every dude at my gym parading around with a big flaccid johnson is a quadrant 4 show-er. Probabilities be damned!

The flaccid to erect johnson relationship is highly complex. To explore it further, I've created another graph from the same two studies which show each study participant's flaccid increase and his flaccid length. This is shown in Figure 44. I've shown all kinds of graphs in this book but in my opinion, this one is the blockbuster.

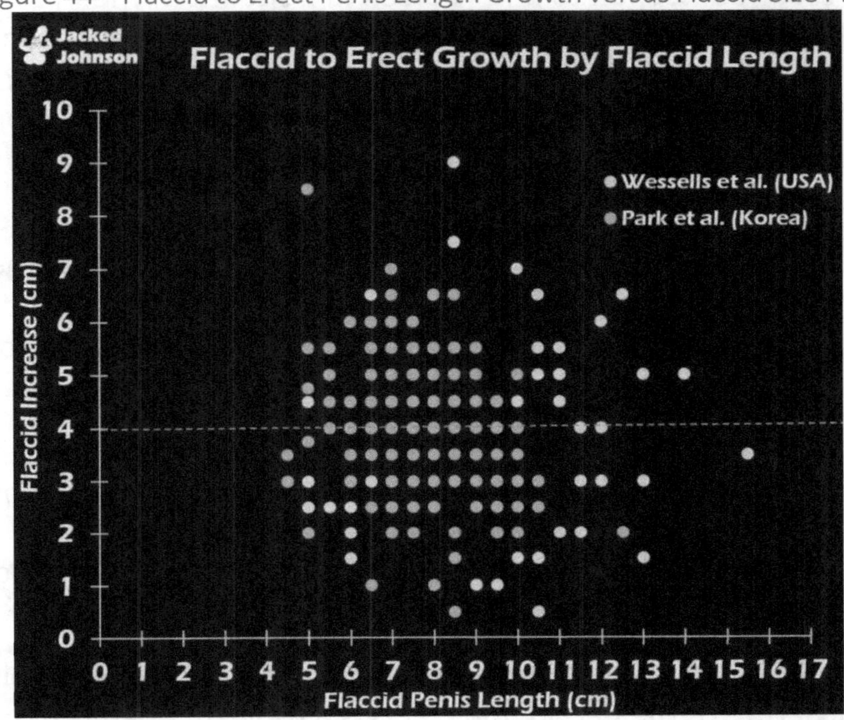

The graph looks like a blood spatter diagram, but that's the beauty of it. The complete randomness of the data points tells us that a man's flaccid length has absolutely no effect on the amount it will increase when erect; literally zero! The coefficient of determination is zero and the regression line is completely flat.

I drew a line on the graph which displays the average absolute increase from flaccid to erect of the two studies, which is 4.05 cm (1.6"). The line almost perfectly cuts the data in half. This means that every flaccid length has roughly the same distribution of growth outcomes. No matter what a man's flaccid size is, his johnson is going to increase in length by an average of 4 cm when erect. This is downright lunacy!

So if a guy has a flaccid johnson 2 cm longer than your flaccid johnson, chances are that his johnson is going to stay 2 cm longer when you're both erect…in case you happen to find yourself in a situation when you're simultaneously erect with the same guy….hey, I don't ask questions! You do you, man. Figure 44 tells us there's a decent chance that you end up the same size or larger than this guy when push comes to shove (or flaccid comes to stiff). However, on average, the amount you start ahead or behind will remain the same when it's sexy time.

It's baffling to me that a guy hung like a rosebud has the exact same odds of johnson length increase outcomes as a guy with a firehose sized johnson. What happened to proportionality? Where is this 4 cm coming from, rosebud dicks?

Since flaccid to erect growth is an exercise in stretching something from an existing flaccid base, I assumed that the guy with the firehose johnson simply has more to work with. When his flaccid penile skin and components stretched, it would naturally amount to a lot more growth than the guy stretching his rosebud.

The apparent universal 4 cm length increase is just another example of the enigmatic nature of the flaccid dong. This is a topic that needs to be studied more in depth as its confounding to explain scientifically. I'm just spitballing here, but the mitigating factor in johnson growth could be blood flow. No matter how it hangs flaccid, perhaps the human body is only comfortable giving a healthy man about 40 cc of blood for an erection. Do with it what you will, cocksman!

The consistent growth across the spectrum of flaccid sizes narrows the gap between big and small when erect. I discussed the narrower distribution of erect johnson lengths in chapter 10. Figure 45 displays how this works in 3D!

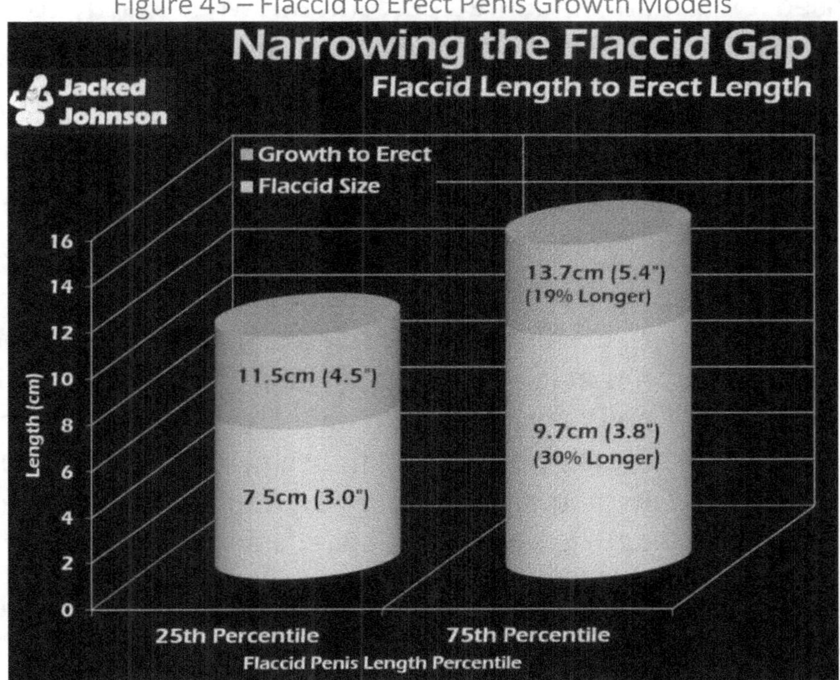

Figure 45 shows a growth comparison of a 25th percentile flaccid length johnson versus one in the 75th percentile. The 75th percentile johnson starts off 30 percent longer in the locker room, but adding the universal average growth of 4 cm, the size gap narrows to only 19 percent in the bedroom. The 75th percentile johnson remains 2.2 cm longer in both states, but on a relative basis, this difference gets reduced significantly i.e. The 25th percentile penis will look a lot less small than the 75th percentile when they're both erect.

What about Growers and Show-ers?

An international men's health survey recently reported that 79% of men believe that their Johnson is a grower (Bean et al, 2006). Of course they do! C'mon!

"Uh...yeah, it grows a lot more than what you see now."

I'm surprised it wasn't one hundred percent. But what exactly constitutes a grower and a show-er? Do we have formal definitions?

Unfortunately, no formal definitions exist; the medical community has failed us! I'm not sure what the survey respondents were basing their answers on. How can any man know which category his johnson falls into? This is critical to know. I guess it's up to me again.

Growers and Show-ers are typically thought of in terms of percentage or relative growth. You're interested in the relative growth from the flaccid base. A flaccid johnson that lengthens significantly from its flaccid base is a grower but what is 'significant'? Fifty percent? One hundred percent? I saw a blog that said seventy percent but they clearly pulled the number right out of their ass. Remember in Figure 39 that the average relative johnson growth for length is 52 percent, so let's entertain the idea of using 50 percent as the Grower/Show-er dividing line.

The tentative definitions that I will be submitting to the World Health Organization are:

Grower: a Johnson that grows more than 50 percent in length from the flaccid to erect state.

Show-er: a Johnson that grows less than 50 percent in length from the flaccid to erect state.

Figure 46 displays the relative growth of the 367 Johnsons in the Wessells et al. and Park et al. studies.

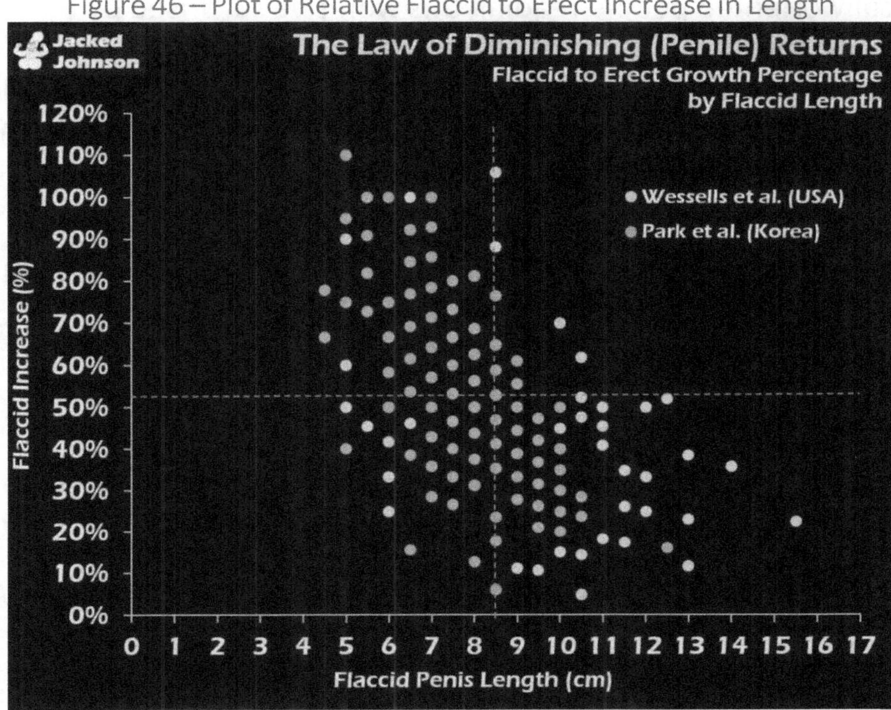

The graph shows that relative johnson growth has a negative relationship with flaccid length. In other words, the longer a guy's flaccid penis is, the less it's expected to grow on a relative basis. You can see that it's the below average flaccid johnson sizes putting up the big growth figures, with several doubling in length. Almost all of the locker room heroes with above average flaccid johnsons grow less than 50 percent, with many barely growing at all. How about that for evening the score? Mother Nature is a mad scientist!

What Figure 46 also exposes how foolish it is to use percentage growth as the basis for determining Growers and Show-ers. According to my now asinine definitions, Growers are just guys with below average flaccid size. Men with above average flaccid johnsons would basically all be deemed Show-ers. Sounds good to me! Great definitions! You're welcome! Goodnight everybody!

Statistically oriented people reading this won't be surprised by <u>Figure 46</u>. If every flaccid johnson big or small is growing about 4 cm, then on a percentage basis that 4 cm is much more significant to smaller flaccid johnson e.g. 4 cm divided by 4 cm is 100 percent growth, while 4 cm divided by 12 cm is 33 percent growth.

In light of these findings, and taking heed of what we learned about absolute johnson growth, it actually makes a lot more sense to use 4 cm as the cut off value. So if a man's johnson grows more than 4 cm, he's a grower! If his johnson grows less, he's a Show-er. Nice and simple!

So to recap our new definitions are:

Grower: a Johnson that grows more than 4 cm (1.6") in length from flaccid to erect.

Show-er: a johnson that grows less than 4 cm (1.6") in length from flaccid to erect.

A Nobel Prize in medicine could be in this author's future! Figure 47 shows a graph of flaccid length versus erect length with each johnson newly defined as a Grower or Show-er.

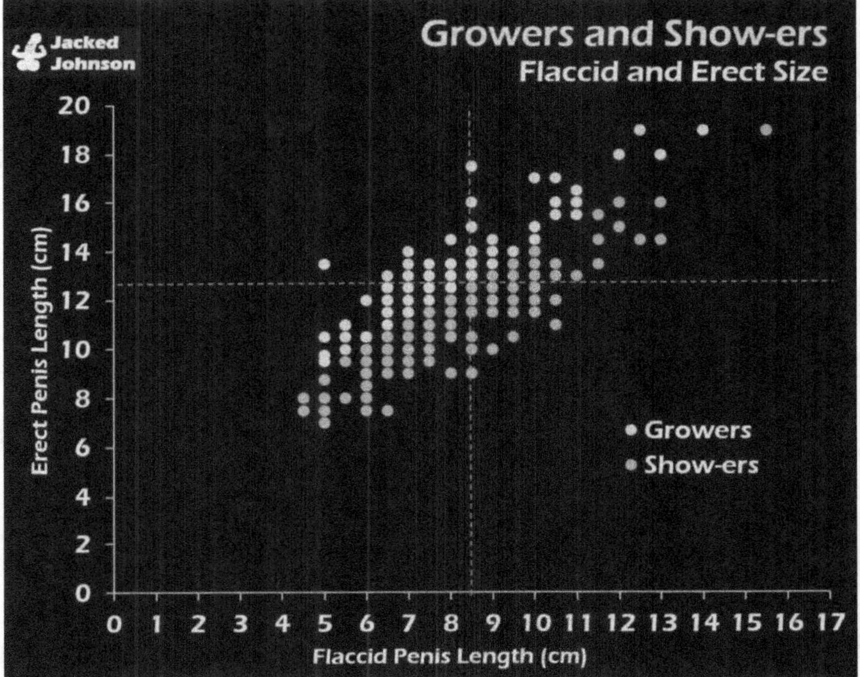

The graph shows what's essentially an even split of Growers and Show-ers at every flaccid johnson length. I feel better about these definitions, as they are more democratic and effectively evaluate above and below average johnson growth.

Part V: Microjohnson

12

How small is too small? Defining the Micropenis

Who doesn't love a good micropenis joke? The scientific term has recently entered into everyday vernacular, commonly inserted into jokes amongst male friends trying to reference somebody's alleged very small penis. The term has definitely been well utilized in my group of friends.

But what does micropenis really mean? And what are the criteria for having one? Surprisingly, these questions don't have simple answers and defining the condition has provd difficult and controversial.

At its core, the term micropenis defines a penis that is *abnormally small but otherwise perfectly formed*. It's caused primarily by a defect in androgen synthesis and androgen response during a critical phase of in utero development. It can also be acquired from injury and disease, so be careful who you make fun of! Karma's a bitch, as they say.

A proper and consistent definition of micropenis is critical but unfortunately has proved elusive. It's important to be diagnosed with micropenis as soon as possible as it's a potential corollary to serious genetic and endocrine issues. Relating specifically to johnson size, the sooner microjohnson is diagnosed, the greater likelihood of success in restoring it within the normal size range. This is usually accomplished via testosterone treatment before a boy hits puberty.

Misdiagnosis of micropenis has resulted in everything from boys being surgically transformed to and raised as girls, to adult men getting their johnsons butchered in a warehouse in Brazil by a doctor with a medical degree written in crayon. So yea, the stakes are very high. But what's the difference between a guy simply getting one of the shorter straws in the genetic johnson lottery--the same type of lottery every one of us enters into for attributes like height, looks, and intelligence--and a more serious problem?

Height, or stature, is a good parallel to the microjohnson. Think about the situation parents face with a very short child. Is the kid just on the shorter end of the height spectrum or do they need to intervene? The Food and Drug Administration considers children shorter than 2.25 standard deviations less than the mean for kids the same age and gender to be 'abnormally short', or to have 'idiopathic short stature' (ISS). In other words, the child is in the shortest 1.2 percent of the population. But even with something as fundamental as height, there isn't uniformity. Other researchers and medical professionals have advised using 2.0 standard deviations.

I'm surprised at these somewhat arbitrary definitions. The average adult male in developed countries is about 5 foot 10 inches tall, with a standard deviation of 2.5 inches. This means that if we use the 2 standard deviations definition, any man below 5 foot 5 inches in stature would be considered to be abnormally short. Some notable men falling below that height are legendary actors Danny Devito (reportedly about 4 foot 10) and Joe Pesci (reportedly 5 foot 4). Even Harry Potter himself Daniel Radcliffe is on the brink, with a reported stature of 5 foot 5...and he's a goddamn wizard! Are men below this height unable to live normal lives? I think a lot of guys would trade lives with Joe Pesci. The treatments for idiopathic short stature are potentially unsafe and very expense; so parents and doctors have to be prudent in determining whether it's appropriate to intervene.

Getting back to the johnson, medical interventions to increase johnson size all have their own risks potential expenses. Parents and doctors have to make a similar call as they do with their child's stature. How small is too small? In this author's opinion, at its most basic level, *micropenis for an adult should be an erect penis length that is too small for successful sexual intercourse*. The size when traditional intercourse positions become difficult or impossible should be the cut-off. If the johnson can't do what it was designed to do, it's obviously a problem. Anything that gets added to the definition becomes a subjective determination as to what is acceptable to live a normal life, just like with height. I get it though, nobody wants to be in the bottom few percentiles in anything!

Unfortunately, my definition doesn't encapsulate non-adults and that's when it's most critical to define micropenis. Before puberty is when doctors, parents, and patients have the most options for treatment. Proper adult definition is also critical because although treatment options narrow significantly in adulthood, some options like penile enlargement surgery are still viable.

Doctors and urologists have seen a pretty dramatic increase in men pursuing possible surgical options, which remain risky and far from guaranteed to deliver acceptable results (although this is improving). Arming doctors with proper size information is critical so they can properly weigh risks and benefits of surgery with adult patients.

Currently, common micropenis definitions follow a similar lead to ISS. The most widely accepted definition is *a normally formed penis that is shorter than 2.5 standard deviations less than the mean for a given age range.* Another common definition uses 2 standard deviations, which is what's recommended in Wessells et al. Figure 48 is a histogram that displays the two micropenis definitions for erect penis length using the distribution created in this book.

Based on the minus 2.5 SD definitions, it results in a cut-off length of 7.69 cm (3.0") and would affect approximately 0.62 percent of adult men. This is close to the erect length of 7.5 cm suggested by Wessells et al. for micropenis. The minus 2.0 standard deviations definition results in a cut-off length of 8.66 cm (3.4") and would affect about 2.1 percent of men.

A study published in 2011 in the British Journal of Urology International (Khan et al, 2011) added some additional perspective on the micropenis issue. This study measured over 600 British men's johnsons in the flaccid and stretched states. Based on their analysis, using minus 2.5 standard deviations from the mean resulted in a micropenis threshold of 10.1 cm in the *bone-pressed* stretched and erect state. However, the authors described the same concerns about arbitrarily defining micropenis that I do. In their professional opinion, a bone-pressed erect penis length of approximately 10 cm (3.9") could begin to cause functional problems for standard intercourse positions. Subtracting the mean pubic fat pad calculated in the study of 1.5 cm (0.6"), it results in a non bone-pressed erect length of about 8.5 cm (3.4"). This cut-off value would affect about 1.8 percent of adult men. The 8.5 cm number is far from definitive and warrants further investigation, but it's a definitely a step in the right direction.

The two prevalent definitions based on are displayed in Figure 48. The 8.5 cm cut off derived from the BJUI study would fall just under the -2.0 SD value.

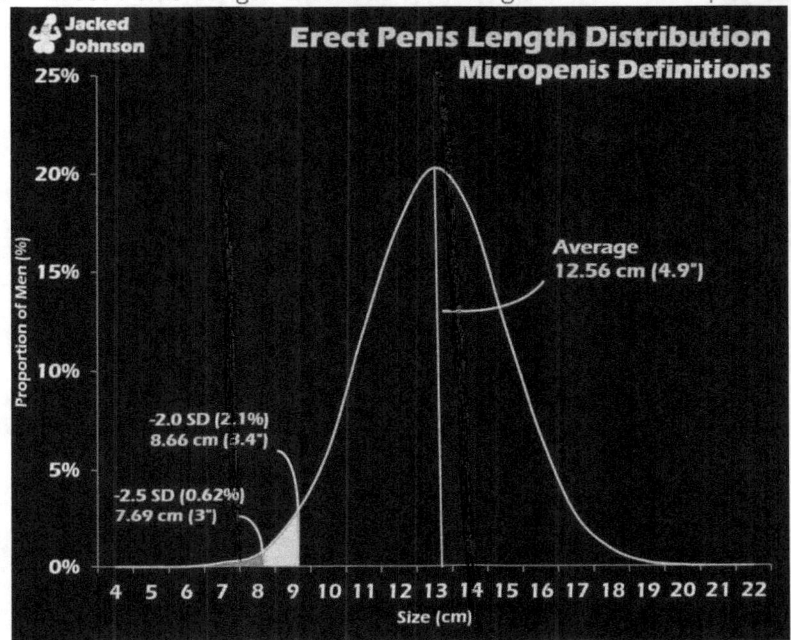

If 2.5 standard deviations less than the mean is being defined as abnormally small in many research papers, then plus 2.5 standard deviations away from the mean must be abnormally *large*. Based on the distribution, a man with an erect johnson longer than 17.4 cm or 6.9 inches can consider himself to be abnormally large. Congratulations to the insufferable assholes above that threshold. Just kidding. Uh…I mean… congratulations…to myself!

I also performed the same micropenis determination for the flaccid johnsons. You can never forget about the flaccid johnson! Like I mentioned in chapter 7, more men are concerned with improving the size of their flaccid johnson only so this is important to define correctly. The values are shown in Figure 49.

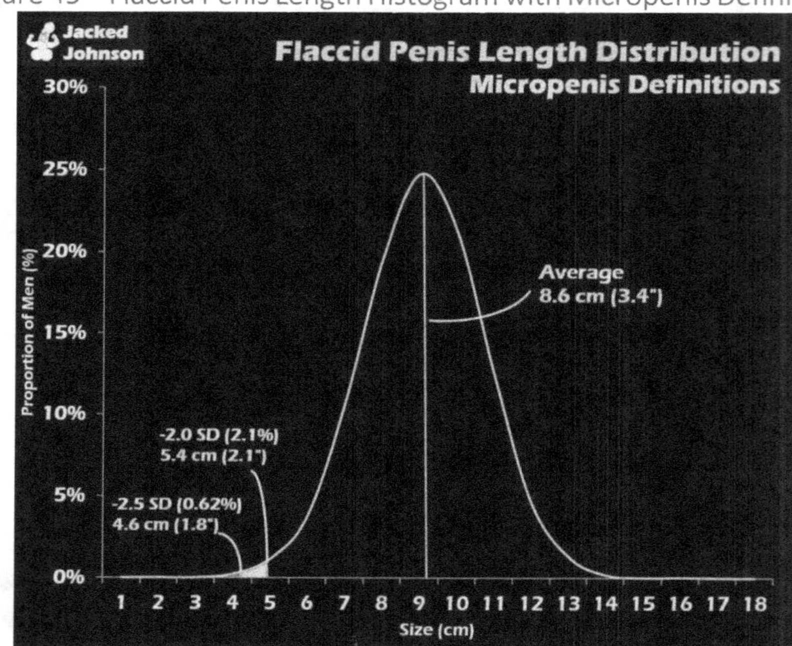

Based on the minus 2.5 SD definition, a flaccid johnson length less than 1.8 inches or 4.6 cm, should be considered for micropenis. This is slightly above the 4.0 cm (1.6") threshold provided in Wessells et al. but just under the 4.7 cm (1.9") detailed in the previously mentioned BJUI study by Khan et al.

Moving to the other side of the distribution, a flaccid length longer than 11.2 cm or 4.4 inches would be considered abnormally large. Congratulations to these locker room legends.